Religious Myth Buster

Escape to Grace

Deon Stevens

Revised edition of Religious Myth Buster

ISBN 978-0-620-46392-8
Copyright ©2015 by Deon Stevens

Published by Deon Stevens

www.deonstevens.wordpress.com

Contents

THANKS

My sincere thanks to Charles Mercer for applying his artistic flair to the design of the cover. I am so grateful to God for putting us together as friends, mountain trail trekkers, grace junkies and fellow religious myth busters. I wonder how things would have turned out if our paths had not crossed at a time when we were left battered and bruised by abusive religion.

And to Sue Smid whose understanding of grace and invaluable help with proof reading is very much appreciated. I take full responsibility for any grammatical errors that may have crept in—I could not resist a last-minute temptation to tamper and tweak.

And most of all to my darling wife, Susan, for loving me. You have had a myth busting husband locked away in his study from dusk till dawn for months on end, paying more attention to busting myths than to being with you. I love you sweetheart!

This book is dedicated to those
who have difficulty accepting
what religion has made of our
relationship with God

PREFACE

This book carries a cautionary notice: You might not appreciate your religion being put under a microscope. What if your many years of sincere religious observances are found to be without substance? Would you be brave enough to kick them into touch? If you were to discover that God has made a religious-less way of fellowshipping with Him, would you allow your religion to keep you from it?

If, after reading this first paragraph, you are still reading—this book will take you on a journey with me in a frank evaluation of what we as believers are often caught up with in our sincere attempts to obtain more of God's favour. It seems so pious to strive for religious acceptance, but it is not our righteous making efforts that earn favour; it is our faith.

Often, the enemy of grace is not the sinner; it is the saint. To many saints, grace seems too easy going to be religious enough. But the way of grace does not only stand up to scriptural scrutiny—there simply is no other way to have a relationship with God. It has to be one or the other: Grace and grace alone, or nothing at all!

The insights of this book are not the way-out eccentric imaginations of a pot smoking saint—each insight was developed out of the black eyes and bruises acquired in the often rough and tumble mismanaged world of church governance. But this book is not about the wounds of church wars; it is about an alternative life—a life more loved! Abusive church authority that could have left me scarred and disfigured, instead drove me to discover a field in which treasure is buried. I have sold everything I own in order to buy this field. The treasure is the knowledge of how unconditionally God loves us!

Each person's perception of the depth of heavenly Father's love is unique and different, making for unique and different depths of relationships. If our denomination has drawn the line on His love at any point short of unconditionality, tragically, we have been defrauded!

Here is where it all goes horribly wrong! We tend to project our misunderstandings of God's loves onto our interpersonal relationships. If we see Him as harsh and judgemental, we are likely to be just as harsh and judgemental towards each other. The way that we experience everyday life is firmly rooted in what we understand of God's undying love for us.

By the time that you turn the last page, my hope is that you'll have a greater insight into the depths of God's love for you, and that this will empower you to live a life of divine companionship and favour in a way that you may never have dreamt possible!

Let's be perfectly honest—everybody benefits from love. And without question, nothing is more compelling than unconditional love! His love is not meted out to us in accordance with our participation in religious programmes, doctrinal formulas, pious activities, denominational dogma, or adherence to a particular order of service. Like bells and smells, our actions cannot convince God to love us one iota more. How can they? He already loves us completely! Seriously, did you really get that? If He loved us enough to die for us while we were lost in sin, can you for moment imagine that He would love us any less now that He has made us holy? Let's face it—nobody can claim that their actions caused Him to love them.

Before we did anything worthy of love, He had already made up His mind to love the entire sin cursed world, to the extreme extent of dying for it[41]. The "world" includes everybody on the planet, whether pious or not. How glorious is that? We can relax—we are loved without regard for our weak, and often faltering attempts at holy living.

Although He loves us regardless, sadly, many sincere believers forego their blood bought privileges, never getting to luxuriate in them. This perfect love affair is only enjoyed by those who are convinced that God's love comes without strings attached. Those who have made this discovery need no persuasion—they know that graceless religion is a myth! We simply do not have to achieve a certain level of holy living to get God's attention—our best attempts at piety cannot persuade Him to love us one iota more than He already does. That's because He loves us completely!

If after reading this book, you come to decide that your religious practises are hampering, rather than enhancing intimacy with your divine Lover, you will be faced with the question, "Am I brave enough to take a leap of faith from meaningless religiousness, into the waiting arms of a loving Dad?" If I choose to stay with religion's many myths, could I ever find contentment in its unachievable demands? Let's be honest, a divine relationship that rests on what I am doing for Him, can never be as dependable as a relationship that rests on what He has done for me!

AN UNABASHED MYTH BUSTER

Myths, urban legends and old wives tales can be fascinating, even amusing; unless of course, we get ensnared in the web of their fallacies. When we are convinced that our particular bent on religion is the last say on the matter, we are unlikely to entertain the notion that our cherished dogma could be keeping us out of something as sublime as a divine romance with the King of kings. But if our security lies in something that is as insecure as our actions, then our fascination with myths and legends is no longer a laughing matter!

When it comes to graceless religion, I am unashamedly a myth buster. Understandably, this does not always go down too well with sincere religious folk. What can I say? Like Charlie Brown's security blanket toting best friend, Linus, nobody enjoys having other people meddle with their cherished comforts. Personal convictions and beliefs are usually guarded and out of bounds to stirrers; let alone myth busters!

When our security stands on religion, we are not standing on very secure ground, yet many choose to trust their own ability to keep the rules of religion, rather than to trust in the undeserved favour and love of God.

Those who choose religion have chosen a difficult path—how can they ever be sure that they have done enough religion? The short answer is that they have never done enough. Anything short of perfection is simply not enough, and let's be honest, mortals are incapable of perfection. The reality is that many sincere believers completely miss out on a courtship with Jesus. They have been cautioned to be weary of something their leaders have labelled "sloppy agape", and consequently are excluded from participating in the glory of a divine romance. If only they knew that there is far more certainty in God's unmerited favour, than in humanity's fallible resolve to keep rules, life would be gloriously different for them. God's love is infinitely more trustworthy than mankind's feeble attempts at staying the course. How often haven't our sincerest promises to live right ended up on the scrapheap of good intentions?

Please understand, I am not a myth buster by choice—my personal religious bubble was burst at a time when my doctrinal views were at the very core of who I was. Like most people in my denomination, my personal convictions were not negotiable, period—or so I thought! When I began to see God's love in a completely different light, I knew that I had to put aside religion's inflexible dogmas in order to obtain the prize of a life more loved. Actually, I was already more loved; I just hadn't understood that I didn't have to do anything special to deserve it. My very best efforts to earn more of His love were done in vain—nothing more than valuable time squandered on religious pointlessness. At first, I found the process of giving up my cherished doctrines and holy cows to be very painful, but for as long as I held onto them, I could not even begin to understand the extent of God's love for me.

Since my discovery, and subsequent liberation from a performance-based relationship, how could I, in all good conscience, keep it to myself? God does nothing by half measures—when it comes to love, He loves completely!

Scores of believers, who honestly try to earn His favour, are often exasperated by their weak and ineffective efforts—the favour they so earnestly seek, always seems to be just beyond their reach. Their breathless pursuing, their to-ing and fro-ing to impress Him, their jostling hither and thither for brownie points, their efforts to fix themselves, just never seems to do the trick. So they beat themselves half to death with self-condemnation for missing the mark. All this mad scrambling for more of God, albeit in complete sincerity, serves only to prove that they don't understand how complete they are in Christ. Even if they never do another thing to impress God, they remain entirely accepted and completely loved just as they are. From the actions of so many sincere believers, it is clear that they do not understand from what it is that Christ has liberated them.

I am a perfect example of one who was uncompromisingly committed to religious conformity—obediently doing my best to implement the steps outlined in each sermon. I felt duty bound to try to please God sufficiently, hoping to stay in His good books. I found myself forever floundering for favour, but sadly, never having much to show for my efforts. My problem was simple—I had not grasped the depth of God's love for me. Thankfully, that all changed on the day of a business meeting. It was just an ordinary day at work with nothing noteworthy to prepare me for what was about to take place.

I was ushered into a businessman's office. With his hand over the telephone mouthpiece, he interrupted his phone call to greet me. Pointing to a seat, he excused himself for continuing with the call. I became so bored waiting for the call to end, that I picked up a book lying on his desk, opened it randomly and began to read.

I had no idea that this ordinary day was about to become an appointment with destiny—a 'Kairos moment'! The first sentence that I aimlessly began reading caused me to sit up and take notice.

"Nothing that I can do can make God love me more, and nothing that I can do can make Him love me less." Wow! How profound! How enormously insightful! How life transforming! How dazzling was the thought of being so unconditional loved! One short sentence, more impactful than a lifetime of sermons. "Religious busting" words running contrary to my treasured religious paradigms.

This led me to turn from religion to a life more loved! Divine courtship soon took on new meaning, propelling me to new levels of intimacy—another dimension of divine romance!

I didn't know then that a greater impact was yet to come. First there was a time of confirming this idea in the scriptures, then allowing the thought of being so completely loved to sink in. Just accepting this truth was enormously edifying—almost intoxicating! How could I have known so much about God, yet misunderstood how dearly and unconditionally I was loved? I had no idea that these few profound words would stir up a compulsion within me to spread God's good tidings. I always battled to find enthusiasm for school essays, yet I cannot stop writing about the good news of His love. What was it that had ignited this passion within me? Nothing other than a fresh understanding of the gracious love of our dear Father!

This was the information that I had so desperately needed. It brought an end to my diligent scrambling for religious scores to impress God.

If religion were to disclose how unconditionally we are loved, religion would immediately lose its reason to exist.

Perhaps you share my frustrations with religion—many do! In all honesty, religion must be seen for what it is. The enemy has hijacked the gospel to suit his own twisted agenda. He has made it his business to side-track God's beautiful children—keeping them busy with seemingly good religion—it's how he keeps believers out of God's glorious grace. But with all that religion promises, it remains a gazillion miles short of the good that God has planned for us.

Yes, religion does offer a beautiful bouquet of promises, but beware; the effort required of us to earn God's favour is endless, and ultimately futile—unrealised dreams eventually take their toll on our confidence. The fruitlessness of it all can so easily leave us with a sense of defeat—unfulfilled dreams lead to feelings of unworthiness.

When prayers are answered, religion will convince us to take credit for the part we played in pleasing God in some way. When someone experiences God's intervention, we may be quick to point out that we prayed and fasted for them—how self-satisfying to steal the glory!

We have come to believe that, when things go well, it is because we have done something to give God reason to love us more. Then when things don't go our way, we get the impression that we have done something to cause Him to turn against us. Unless we discover that He loves us through thick and thin, just as much when we have failed to do good, as when we have done good, we will have a yo-yo relationship—never quite knowing where we stand with Him. He doesn't love us because of something that we have or have not done—He loves us because He is love—incapable of anything less[114]!

Religion always has us on a short leash—never allowing us to be honest with ourselves. We dare not admit that our religious efforts are fruitless, lest other believers mistake our honesty for spiritual weakness—our struggle must at all times appear to be victorious; our defeats must remain secret—our religious reputations are at stake!

So we resort to dishonesty. Something without which we would be vulnerable to the surreptitious criticism of religious compatriots. With religion, appearances are everything! In our efforts to gain the respect of leadership, we find ourselves masking our weaknesses. The higher we are promoted in spiritual circles, the less we are allowed to be ourselves. Although, in all likelihood entirely unintentional, religion's impossible expectations force us to adopt hypocrisy for the sake of appearances.

Many ministers lead very lonely lives—their faultless images must always appear to be without blemish. They may have serious inner struggles, yet feel obliged to keep them secret for fear of losing face.

How sad! If only they knew—people identify with struggles—no one is immune from them. Transparency is not a sign of weakness; it is a sign of virtue. It's a fact of life—people find it easier to identify with honesty than with pretence! Yes, there might be secrets that are too dark to share with the congregation, but there is no judgement in genuine friendship; only empathy and compassion. Sadly, once religious standards have been imposed, there is no place left for empathy.

Isn't it just so sad—our contrived efforts to appear perfect serve only to keep the very ones who could help us get through our personal struggles, at arm's length? Without question—it takes transparency to be real. Good old-fashioned honesty trumps religious shamming any day of the week! Let's call it what it is: In portraying something that we are not, we are no more than "hypocrites"! Hiding our weaknesses for the sake of finding acceptance makes relationships shallow. Openness on the other hand is very different, and thankfully, comes with a handsome payoff!

Pretence can only be taken so far. In a moment of weakness, we are apt to let our guards down, and suddenly our secret struggles become obvious to all. Even insignificant issues can at times be blown out of all proportion as the church's gossip mongers add their exaggeration before broadcasting it to others under the religious pretext of "sharing". Inflated news spreads like wildfire, as every last juicy detail is eagerly devoured, added to and piously passed on. You may get a phone call that goes something like, "We thought that you ought to know what's happened so that you can pray for so and so". The news that follows is usually shocking, as every last juicy detail is piously spiced up and doused in sauce. Sadly, once the beans have been spilled, they cannot be un-spilled.

Infuriation or liberation—the choice is yours. What a shame it would be if the words of this book so infuriate you that you miss a golden opportunity to be liberated from the affliction of burdensome religiosity. In religious circles, we don't always understand why we do what we do—often it is just the done thing, and nobody seems to complain. Sometimes, the things we do to obtain God's favour, are the very things that obstruct His favour.

Somebody said that for years it puzzled him as to why his wife always cut off both ends of the beef fillet before putting it in the oven. He feared that it may have its roots in superstition, so he decided to ask her. She replied that she didn't know why she did it, but it was something that her mother always did. Wanting to get to the bottom of this odd custom, he asked her mother, and to his surprise, she also didn't know why she did it, except that it was something that her mother had always done. Now really curious, he went to her mother to get to the bottom of it. For the first time he got a proper explanation. She did it because her oven was too small to take the whole fillet. Amazingly, grandma's daughter and granddaughter had made a tradition out of grandma's problem. This problem had no relevance to grandma's offspring—both of them had large enough ovens to take the whole fillet untrimmed.

There are things that we do in our spiritual walks that have no relevance whatsoever. Just as part of the fillet was lost, so we lose part of God's good intentions towards us. Our religious paradigms may seem harmless enough, but if they are getting in the way of a divine romance, are they really worth the trouble?

I have agonised over how I should bring to the attention of believers the church's subtle departure from the radical grace that Paul so passionately advocated. How can I tell of the dangers without exposing the misguidedness of it all? It is a given—individuals caught up in these practices are likely to take offence, but I assure you, no offence is intended.

If I don't tell it like it is, I have no right to expect you to read this book. If I do tell it like it is, some may take it personally. But if the story must be told, it must be told the way I know it. As I draw from personal experiences, I mention personalities involved in forming my perspectives. I have taken special care not to identify them—it is not my intention to embarrass anybody. To water my story down any further would be dishonest and disrespectful to you the reader.

Every experience involves characters, and none of these characters are bad people; they are good people caught up in something religious, in all likelihood passed down to them from respected men of God. They are convinced that their way is the only way, and I respect them for sticking to their convictions.

If you find reason in these pages to take offence, please accept my sincere apology in advance. I bear no malice against anybody mentioned. Prompt forgiveness is something that I have learnt through the University of Hard Knocks. I simply cannot afford the mistaken luxury of indulging in unforgiveness. I love the concept of mercy, and am convinced that there is ample mercy for all parties involved, including myself, a man patently aware of his many shortcomings.

Take care to not mistake my criticism of religious systems, to be criticism of God's beloved family. We are all part of His glorious church. His love for "her" is obvious—having laid His life down for "her". I tread softly out of respect for both Him and His treasured bride. I am profoundly aware of His deep affection for her. He jealously guards her from accusers. And that's why my criticisms are not aimed at denominations, church leaders or believers; they are aimed at religious systems and graceless paradigms that have robbed innocent followers of Jesus of their blood bought privileges.

When John was in the Spirit on the Isle of Patmos, he saw the Son of man standing among the seven churches. These churches were depicted as "golden" candle sticks. As much as gold depicts flawless value, He went on to reveal that these churches were not without flaws. In associating them with gold, He expressed just how valuable and precious they are to Him. It is significant to note that their failings did not reduce their value—they remained every bit as good as gold in His estimation.

The words of this book come out of my concern for those of God's highly valued children, who have become ensnared in religious entanglements at the expense of a sublime romance with the King of kings.

As you read these pages, I trust that you will prayerfully consider whether your spiritual paradigms are "religious" by nature, or "grace" by nature. I shall do my best to make the distinction clear.

Happy reading!

A BUNCH OF SCRUFFS

I was shocked, confused, bewildered
As I entered Heaven's door,
Not by the beauty of it all,
Nor the lights or its decor.

But it was the folks in Heaven
Who made me splutter and splash,
The thieves, the liars, the sinners,
The alcoholics and the trash.

There stood the kid from seventh grade
Who swiped my lunch money twice.
Next to him was my old neighbour
Who never said anything nice.

Herb, who I always thought
Was rotting away in hell,
Was sitting pretty on cloud nine,
Looking incredibly well.

I nudged Jesus, 'What's the deal?
I would love to hear Your take.

How'd all these sinners get up here?
God must've made a mistake.

'And why is everyone so quiet,
So sombre—give me a clue?'
'Hush, child,' He said, 'they're all in shock.
No one thought they'd be seeing you.' [86]

We might be a shabby bunch of scruffs, but fortunately, our scruffiness does not reduce us in God's sight. Our status is that of glorious sons and daughters of the most-high God, and that status cannot be reduced by our raggedness. Some of us are more raggedy than others—it's a case of degrees—we are a ragtag bunch of believers, and that goes for the best of us.

When we finally come to the point where we feel free enough to admit to our bedraggled-ness, we finally come to the point where we get real! Real people do not have to parade and posture. But it is different for religious people—they dare not be real—it would be equivalent to admitting to their bedraggled-ness. But here's the deal—bedraggled yet loved—normal people living in abnormal favour!

In striving for appearance's sake, what are we making of our Christianity? Could we have slipped back into the very fraudulence from which we have been saved? Is it any wonder that those looking in identify religiousness as hypocrisy? But sadly, Christians just don't seem to get it!

The very reason for Christ's coming, was to take into account that we are a raggedy bunch, and to make up for our raggediness with His very own righteousness; not ours! The righteousness that He imputes to us is not something that we can boast about—it is all His doing[66].

With holy posturing and pious pretending, we do our best to conform to what religion expects of us. We feign holiness, oblivious to the enemy's tactic of keeping our Christianity shallow. He takes full advantage of our artificialities for his own devious purposes.

As sincere as our efforts may be, they do not make us one iota more righteous than we already are. In God's estimation, we are every bit as righteous as Jesus[77]! Our sincerest efforts are always below par—they can never equal holiness. Holy actions are Holy Spirit inspired actions called fruit of the Spirit.

Sadly, as commendable as clerical oversight is, sincere submission to leadership is sometimes misused to wield undo control over believers. Clerical abuse is nothing new to the church; it has been going on for countless centuries. God has appointed shepherds, and they ought to be trusted. But unfortunately, there are shepherds and there are shepherds. Those who lead in the spirit of servanthood, and those who manipulate in the spirit of dictatorship! Obviously, the freedom that comes with grace presents a threat to control freaks— grace simply cannot be policed! Yet there are many who feel duty bound to pull strings as though congregants are puppets—they will do whatever it takes to enforce their version of "holiness". Beware! Religion without grace is a cult in the making!

The principle of fathering and discipleship is God's idea—vital to the spiritual health and wellbeing of the body of Christ. Fathering is sublimely edifying when done God's way. Obviously, one cannot generalise, but there is an unfortunate form of religious fathering that oversteps the mark. Beware! The moment fathering becomes controlling, discipleship is headed for Christian cultism—a religious calamity!

Our antennae should at all times be on the alert. Cults often start out innocently enough, and at first seem no different to any other church on the block. But beware of dictatorial figures who demand blind obedience to their lofty religious ideas, and subservience to their self-exalted rank in the religious pecking order. When this happens, it is time to be afraid! History is littered with tragic outcomes of dutiful submission to domineering father figures.

To name but a few of the more well-known religious cults that have ended in tragedy: Reverend Jim Jones and The People's Temple resulted in over nine hundred suicides. David Koresh and the Branch Davidians resulted in ninety deaths. The order of the Solar Temple resulted in seventy-four deaths. Heaven's Gate resulted in thirty-nine suicides. The Church Of The Lamb Of God resulted in twenty-four deaths.

Most cultish leaders go through life as meek and mild pastors. They manage to stay under the radar by passing themselves off as benign caring father figures. You wouldn't know what lies beneath their kindly demeanours. At least not until someone dares to question their brand of theology.

You may not fall prey to such devilish devotion, but there are many other religious entrapments set to ensnare innocent devotees.

Religion convinces its followers to make themselves right. Paul pulled no punches—he had a word for it, he called it witchcraft.5 It happens innocently enough, but its end is entrapment to a life sentence of submission to a list of do's and don'ts. Unfortunately do's and don'ts only deal with surface behaviour; they are too superficial to deal with real problems lurking deep within.

When you are prepared to do whatever it takes to gain God's favour, yet never seem to gain it, sincere friends are likely to counsel you to try even harder. In this way you become even more enslaved to performance. Let's be real—performing for God's favour has no reward. This kind of sincere advice is usually innocently given without realising that a performance based relationship with God serves only to demobilise faith. Faith that relies upon our performance is doomed before it begins, but faith that relies upon God's performance is an entirely different kettle of fish! We are not favoured for our performance; we are favoured for putting faith in our gracious Father's performance!

Something as innocent as a desire to do whatever it takes to gain God's love, can be the very thing that keeps us out of indulging in His love. When we want God's favour badly enough, we'll do whatever we believe is necessary to get it. Sadly, many fall for the myth that it can be achieved with religious effort. But in performing for it, we miss out on the sheer pleasure of indulging in what He has provided undeservedly. Of course, once we are entirely assured that we already have all of His love, there is no further need to perform for it.

Religion lays down a set process for finding favour with God— rules abound—specific steps to gain better health, wealth, relationships and happiness. Beware though! When things don't work out the way religion would have us believe they should, disillusion soon follows.

That's no problem for religion—it offers perfectly good explanations as to why things have not worked out as planned. Stock clichés are tritely dished out to get around any doubts gained through disappointments. How often have we heard the words,

"God is not at fault, He wants you to have all these wonderful benefits, so the fault must lie with you. You just didn't do enough to please Him, or there is something about your life that must be straightened out before you can expect Him to favour you." These fallacies keep us trying all the harder, and then even harder when our added efforts don't work out—the quest is endless!

When we are on a religious treadmill, we are unlikely to notice that we are working hard at going nowhere. No matter how much effort we put in, no matter how hard we run, we don't seem to make any headway. Like a hamster, always busy running in his wheel, we are stuck in one place, trapped in the confines of our religious hamster wheels. If we dare to be honest with ourselves, we have to admit that religion's many promised rewards, more often than not, remain just beyond our grasp.

The good news is that you are not at fault. It's not a case of what you have or haven't done; it's a case of understanding how God relates to you, and how profoundly simple it is to relate to Him. If we gained our relationship with Him simply because we feared the dire consequences of not doing so, we will forever be driven by fear, when we should be drawn by love. Consider for a moment: Is it really possible to have a loving relationship with a person holding a gun to our heads? I don't think so!

The problem with a fear-based relationship is that our behaviour is only held on the straight and narrow by the last dose of fear we swallowed on Sunday. Just as a junky must have his next fix to keep his shaky sanity intact, so it is for the pious follower of misguided religion—he depends on his next fix of guilt and condemnation to keep him honest. He cannot afford to risk putting his hope in God's love alone. Another dose of guilt and condemnation is needed to keep his behaviour in check.

When the balance between fear and trust tips in favour of fear, we have wandered away from Jesus' grace. Those who are caught up in a fear-based relationship may even be able to defend such a stance by quoting from the book of Proverbs, saying that fear is the beginning of wisdom. Far be it from me to disagree with such a wise old sage as King Solomon—only a fool would! Interestingly, Solomon discovered fear to be only the beginning of wisdom—it's where wisdom starts—a wisdom that drives us to the point of seeking a solution to our fearful predicament. When we discover that there is a

God who so desperately wants to become our Father and friend, that He would not allow anything to stand in the way, what is there to be afraid of? Fear simply cannot withstand the immensity of God's overwhelming love for us[63]. For a believer who has discovered his or her position as a dearly loved child in God's family, the fear of the Lord is no longer a scary fear, but rather awe and respect for His supreme lordship over them and their every decision. This kind of fear cannot be described as a terrifying fear. Earthly dads are defenders of their families, and our heavenly Father is no different—He is not out to get us; He is out to protect, heal and prosper us!

The horror of hell is often proclaimed to frighten people into holiness. But it should be obvious that when relationships are fear driven, they are not love inspired.

One of the strongest reasons given for entering into a relationship with God is found in John 3:16. In this magnificent scripture, Jesus made no mention of the dreadfulness of hell, but had plenty to say about the depths of God's love for us. Coming into the Kingdom on a "love ticket", rather than a "fear ticket", changes everything about how we relate to God. If we were bullied into the kingdom, then we will forever need bullying to keep us on the straight and narrow. But bullying is not something that Jesus does. That's the work of religion!

Jesus loves us into the kingdom, and then relates to us with nothing but pure unadulterated love. When getting out of hell becomes our reason for having a relationship with God, then we cannot claim to be in the relationship for any reason other than to serve our selfish interests. With self-centredness, who is it that we are actually serving? Is it God, or ourselves? If we love Him so that we don't go to hell, then we don't love Him for who He really is. Can there be anything shallower than that?

On the other hand, if our decision to follow Christ came about as a result of, firstly, realising our perilous predicament without a saviour, and secondly, realising that God has gone out of His way to love us into His kingdom, then we enter into a relationship based on mutual love for each other. Are we saved from hell's fires? Most certainly! But the dreadfulness of hell should not be the reason for being in the relationship; the gloriousness of heaven in our hearts is reason enough!

A problem arises when religion is our "get out of jail" monopoly card. It allows hell's fires to define our relationship. When our religion stands on our "escape from hell ticket", it does not stand on God's love.

With religion, we continuously ask ourselves, "Am I doing enough? Am I good enough? Is my faith strong enough?" Quite frankly, the answer is always and without exception, no! We are never good enough; we have never done enough; and our faith is never strong enough. Religion will always demand more from us than we can give. We cannot afford to rely on ourselves for any of the afore mentioned. If we dare, we will always, and without exception, come up short.

If, in the first place, we were not good enough and could not do enough to save ourselves, what chance is there that our future doings will be good enough to win God's favour and keep us saved. In as much as our puny efforts could not save us, neither can they favour us nor keep us saved. More church commitments, more converts notched up to our credit, more Bible study, more prayer—all commendable activities in themselves, but no amount of extra commitments can in anyway obligate the God of the entire universe to attend to the whims and fancies of mere mortals. It is not our whims and fancies that motivate Him, He has already obligated Himself—taken on the responsibility of fulfilling all of the required conditions as embedded in His loving covenant of grace. Now the privileges are ours for the asking. This covenant replaced the previous covenant which required people to earn rewards[43].

While our good Christian living is motivated by fear, we will do all kinds of good works for all the wrong reasons. The bottom line is, we can never feel safe in a relationship fuelled by fear. The mere fact that we are fearful is proof enough that we have not discovered the depth of His love for us. Just knowing how perfectly we are loved is immensely edifying. Love casts out all fear[63].

The good news, according to the Bible, is that if God didn't even spare His own son for our sakes, then surely to goodness He will not withhold anything else that is good for us[116]. The reason for not withholding anything from us is not our exemplary performance; it is simply that He is in love with us. Seeing His love has stretched to such an extreme extent, it stands to reason that it won't need any further stretching to include everything else. But surely, He requires holiness of us, doesn't He? Sure He does! But it's not holiness by effort; it's holiness by imputation! When we know what He has imputed to us, there is no further need to be cajoled into holiness; holiness simply turns up in our actions in an unforced way. When we are obeying the gentle guidance of His Spirit within us, fruit of the Spirit appears without effort. Sounds simple enough, but how can we be expected to trust the very One we have been taught to be fearful of? It is simply not possible!

That being the case, we need assurance that our trust is not misplaced. In our minds, our fears are always legitimate—whether the thing feared is real or imagined is immaterial—imagination becomes the way we compute reality—to us our imagination is reality. We cannot just throw out what to us are legitimate fears, and begin to trust. We need to be convinced. In that case, consider the torturous lengths Jesus went to for our sakes on the cross. If that does not convince us, nothing will!

What would it take to make us sufficiently confident to abandon our reservations and throw ourselves at the mercy of another? Would religious commandments do it? I don't think so! Commandments appeal to our dreads, whereas love appeals to our loyalty! His love is not like ours—it is at a level that can always be trusted—it takes no strain when not reciprocated, and doesn't even buckle under betrayal. Not even our foolish straying from Him can cause Him to love us less.

We don't trust just anybody, but we are suckers for love when it comes without reason. If this is not the kind of love you have found in God, you are probably doing your best to prove your worthiness to Him—something that is simply not achievable— nobody's resolve is dependable enough for that!

Relax! His love is not for sale. Though it may not be obvious to us, He sees something immensely lovable in us! And when we discover that we are loved in such a complete way, especially when it comes from the one Person whose opinion really counts, it has a profound effect on the way our lives turn out.

If Christianity were to base its entitlement to God's blessings upon something deserving that we have personally managed to pull off, then Christianity would be just another world religion. What is it that distinguishes Christianity from the religions of the world? The answer to that question is found in one short word:

"grace"! In a nutshell: "favour that is entirely undeserved!" With the religions of the world, god loves righteous people. But with Christianity, God loves unrighteous people. Jesus said that the Father gave His only Son for no reason other than that He so loved the world. The "world"? That's sinners folks! Dirty rotten sinners! He loved them so much that He did not spare His Son in order to save them from the damnation they deserved[41].

No religion, including "religiously modified Christianity", offers anything free of charge. Religions prescribe requirements for the attainment of God's favour—but not so with authentic Christianity! If we have chosen religion, we have chosen a difficult path. In reality, God's blessings and favour are not distributed to the deserving; they are distributed to the expectant. Not a single merit is required.

It is by grace that we are saved; not by personal piety. For if salvation could be attained through good living, we would have reason to boast[83]. That's the problem with religion—the pious find reason for smugness, and before long, they're looking down their noses upon those who struggle with piety.

Conversely, grace does not applaud the pious. It is not for the deserving; it is for the undeserving. Grace is diametrically opposite to rewards—never bestowed when deserved—it is only available to those who are decidedly undeserving. How on earth did religion miss the point? How did undeserved favour mutate into something that must be earned and deserved?

Seeing that Jesus is the founder of Christianity, maybe He would be the best person to defend it. If we were to ask him why He found it necessary to introduce another religion, He would in all likelihood answer, "Me, introduce another religion? You have got to be kidding? The very reason I came was to put a decisive and final end to all that religion is[82]. Your religious observances failed to make you right, so in one fell swoop, I abolished all religious requirements for all time and eternity. I want a real relationship with you, one that is unencumbered by religiousness."

"Well if that's the case Lord, why is Christianity considered to be a religion?"

"It didn't take people too long to reduce a passionate love affair into nothing but a contractual arrangement. It saddened me to see the spontaneity of our courtship slide into nothing more than form and formula. But it is not what you have or have not done that causes Me to love you—I love you just as you are. I don't measure you against a list of do's and don'ts. I inspire obedience with love, and love changes the way you think. Once your thinking has been revolutionised, resistance dissolves and behaviour follows suit."

But surely such reckless love will lead to all kinds of misuse and abuse!

"I am willing to take that risk for the sake of gaining your heart. I am not looking for a pretence of godliness—no amount of human resolve can attain anything remotely resembling holiness. Righteousness is only truly righteous when it is lived out of the righteousness which I imputed to you."[1]

So, what about the ten commandments?

"Because you were not capable of fulfilling them, I fulfilled them for you[2]".

And the Old Covenant? Aren't we blessed for fulfilling the law and cursed for failing to fulfil it?

"God the Father is too just to punish two people for the same crime—I have done your time on the cross so that you don't have to."

Well then, what must I do to avoid the curses and activate the blessings?

"On the cross, I became a curse for all the law that I knew you would fail to fulfil[3]. Now that the curses have been neutralised, the blessings are available to you without merit. You are at liberty to indulge in them; I paid for them with My blood. Delivery of the blessings is not the problem; failure to sign for the delivery is the problem. Don't allow shame to rob you of a blessed life. It takes nothing more than bold faced faith to withdraw divine favour."

They say that there are no free lunches. We are so conditioned to believe that we get nothing for nothing, and religion is no different. Religion requires us to prove our worthiness. But living up to religious expectations is not within the ability of humanity. And when we discover how futile our efforts have been, our self-esteem takes a knock. When our worthiness is brought into question, our confidence falters. But thankfully, His blessings are not awarded in proportion to worthiness; they are gifts, and His gifts can only be received by faith.

In a room of a few hundred people, a speaker started his talk by holding up a bank note. He asked, "Who would like this $100 bill?" Many hands popped up. He said, "I am going to give this bank note to one of you, but first let me do this." He proceeded to crumple the $100 bill in his hand. Then He asked, "Does anybody still want it?" Just as many hands shot up. Well, he replied, "What if I do this?" He dropped it on the floor and began grinding it into the dirt with his shoe. He picked it up all crumpled and dirty. Still just as many hands popped up. No matter what was done to the bank note, the same number of people still wanted it. No matter how crumpled and filthy, its value remained the same—$100.

Often we are dropped, crumpled, and ground into the dirt by the unfortunate decisions we make, and the luckless hand that life sometimes deals us. We may feel worthless, but no matter how shoddily life has treated us, we never lose our value. Dirty or clean, we remain priceless in God's sight. That's because our value is not established by what we have done or who we can boastfully claim to know; our value is established by the One who knows us.

Jesus found you when you were soiled by life's trials and temptations, crushed by the weight of sin, but He still found you to be intensely desirable and hugely valuable—valuable enough to give up His life to redeem you.

If you are feeling drained and battered by life's relentless buffeting—used by uncaring people and worthless to humanity, you should not be evaluating yourself; leave that task to Jesus—He has a much clearer idea of your worth. Judging by the lengths He went to in order to win your heart, you are priceless!

Take heart, God loves you because of who He is; not because of anything you did!

PEOPLE BEFORE CHURCH

At a house church meeting, our leader and his wife asked for prayer. Her parents felt side-lined by their family's overzealous commitment to church activities, thus depriving them of the pleasure of being grandparents.

The home church folk agreed that it was unfair of her parents to put their wants and desires ahead of the church. The group had grown to trust their leaders and appreciated their uncompromising commitment to church activities. "How could her parents be so selfish?"

Sounds reasonable, doesn't it? After all, whenever a job needed to be done, the church could always rely upon this faithful couple to volunteer. Always available—unselfish—generous to a fault—ever ready to sacrifice their leisure for the sake of fulfilling leadership responsibilities. Such wholehearted commitment is rare!

Unfortunately, they had missed the point. Jesus didn't come to establish institutions that distract us from loving each other; He came to reconcile relationships. In as much as we receive His love, gratis and for nothing, we are to give His love away, gratis and for nothing. Jesus did not have barriers in mind; He had the demolishment of barriers in mind. He didn't come to tear down bridges; He came to build bridges! Love begins with those closest to us. There is only one commandment that comes with a promise, and that is the commandment to honour our parents.

In God's order, family and friends come before institutions and organisations. Of course, nothing comes before the King and His kingdom. But we should not confuse religious "institutions" with the kingdom of God—this kind of confusion reduces us from citizens of God's kingdom, to citizens of religious institutions—two vastly different establishments.

In the Bible, the word "church" was not used to describe buildings, denominations or institutions—that's because the original root meaning of the word "church" means a community of people. As hard as it is to imagine, the church of the book of Acts was devoid of institution—believers simply met in homes. These homes were not the church; the members themselves were the church! When, some centuries later, the word "church" was misused to describe religious buildings with pointy windows and steeples, it succeeded only in destroying Jesus' divine romance with His beloved bride, the "church". A raging romance had been reduced to nothing more than a stone-cold relationship with square bricks and dry mortar.

With the precious church of Christ now reduced to nothing more than a stone-cold architectural structure, the excitement of divine romance soon slid into no more than form and formula. As tragic as this was, to this day, many revere their treasured religious affiliations as though God's idea.

This was soon followed by the ecclesiastical tragedy of oversight sliding into clerical control. Before believers could rub the sleep out of their eyes, the clergy had usurped them of their personal priesthood. What followed was a third-party relationship with divinity—a passionate one-on-one love affair exchanged for a detached arm's length arrangement.

When Jesus said, "Everyone who has given up houses or brothers or sisters or father or mother or children or property, for my sake, will receive a hundred times as much in return and will have eternal life"[4], He was not referring to a sacrifice for the sake of an earthly institution; He was referring to a sacrifice for the sake of the Kingdom. God's kingdom exists on earth in the form of God's people—certainly not in the form of buildings, denominations or institutions that bear the name "church" on notice boards.

In the case of our house church leaders, their parents were every bit as much a part of the authentic church of Christ as any other blood washed believer. The kingdom of God consists of ordinary people who have been transformed into extraordinary beings by spiritual rebirth.

If Church programmes get in the way of our relationships with our loved ones, then our participation in them is ungodly.

I have heard that the correct order of priority should be God first, spouse second, children third and church last. While this sounds right, because it correctly places the institutionalised church at the bottom of the list, this kind of prioritising separates God from everything else. God should not be put first—He should be in everything, whether chores or pleasures. What a joy to never have to face anything alone. Our divine Lover really wants to be part of our ups and downs—He understands everything we go through.

Have you noticed how that opening and closing in prayer tends to compartmentalise our lives? It is not even vaguely possible to disconnect from the life of God that is within us—after all, being born of His Spirit makes Him part and parcel of who we are—we exist in Him[126]. Paul calls upon us to pray without ceasing[93]. Our entire existence should be a prayer—Jesus and us, constantly romancing one another.

In partnership with the Holy Spirit, we can confidently face anything that life throws at us. Two is better than one—our eternal oneness with divinity puts us at an unfair advantage. Being joined to almightiness gives us a winning edge in the most devilish of confrontations.

God is not the man upstairs—He is the man downstairs. He has chosen to live inside the scruffiest of us. The fact that He has chosen such shabby dwellings does not subtract from His gloriousness; He remains superbly glorious within us! Jesus said that the glory that God had given Him, He has passed on to us[67]. And it is His glory that we pass on to those around us. He is not ashamed to shine His glory out of the most bedraggled of humanity. God is not uncomfortable with our shortcomings—He wouldn't even notice them unless we told Him about them—He said that He will no longer remember our sins[82]. How immensely privileged we are!

God doesn't want to be first—He loves to be included in everything that we are. His life is inseparable from ours—everything that is of concern to us, is of concern to Him—He appreciates being included in the minutest details of our lives[84]. In His estimation, institutions and their programmes can never be as important as people.

How often haven't we heard sad and regretful tales from people in ministry? They come to the end of a lifetime of selfless service to the work of ministry saying, "If I could do it all over again, I would spend less time in ministry and more time with my family". Church commitments are often the reason that "PKs" (preachers' kids) end up rebelling against the church. Doesn't that tell a story all of its own?

BALANCE DESTROYS GRACE

My father's manager once told me that my dad was a good man with only one flaw—he was too honest. I am not sure that it is possible to be too honest. When honesty is mixed with dishonesty, what do we have? There is only one word for it, and it is not "reasonably honest"—it is plain and simply "full-blown dishonesty". Even the tiniest drop from an eye dropper of dishonesty is enough to obliterate honesty!

Would you employ an accountant to look after your investments if he was relatively honest? Of course, not—that would be insane! How do you think your wife would feel if you were to tell her that you were relatively faithful to her? Understandably, she would have good reason to feel betrayed.

There are certain things in life that when balanced, lose all relevance. Grace is one such commodity. I am often told that my emphasis on grace is too strong and dangerously out of balance, and that over emphasis on any single doctrine leads to error. I am advised to back off on grace and bring grace into balance with holiness.

If you want to bring balance to goodness, what concept would you use to balance it? The one and only concept would be "evil". One pinch of evil mixed with goodness, and goodness is no longer good. When it comes to grace, the undeserved favour of God, what is the one and only concept that could possibly bring balance to it? It can only be "works done in expectation of reward".

When the undeserved favour of God must be earned, it is no longer undeserved, and therefore no longer grace[5]. We have got to make up our minds on this issue—are we saved because we deserve it, or because we don't deserve it? The answer should be obvious. A saviour is not needed for people who are righteous; a saviour is needed for people who are unrighteous. There is no more appropriate description for humanity than the word "unrighteous"! Let's not kid ourselves, we are all a bunch of bedragglers. The same applies to every blessing—we are not healed and favoured because we deserve to be healed or favoured; we are healed because of the stripes upon Jesus' back, and favoured because of His undying love expressed to us upon the cross. It's not our good deeds that bring us favour; it is Jesus' good deeds. It's not about what we did or did not do; it's about what Jesus accomplished for us, period! By faith, we have the privilege of, receiving free gratis and for nothing, everything He achieved for us!

Grace is somewhat like wine—it would be unforgivable to mix a fine ten-year-old bottle of Cabernet Sauvignon with Coca Cola— it must be taken straight.

Mixing a drink of "undeserved grace", with a dash of "trying to deserve it" can be so subtle that the delusion escapes our notice. We may appeal to God for His favour, and patiently wait for an answer. But when the answer is seemingly not forthcoming, we may decide to step in and try to help the process along with some extra church hours, longer quite times, promise to give up something or perform some other Christian duty that we feel would impress God. Before we know it, we have mixed undeserved favour with something that deserves to be rewarded. And that's all it takes to transform a gift into a purchase. Such a transaction would be perfectly acceptable if we could afford the price. The problem is, nobody can—it is far too dear!

Well, what's so wrong with at least trying to deserve something? The problem with that kind of thinking is that rewards are entirely opposite to grace. When we are reward driven, we get to take credit for the part we played, thus stealing the glory that is rightfully God's[83]. The bottom line is, we cannot do enough to deserve any of God's blessings—they are priceless—far too dear for humanity! So why bother trying?

This leads to the question; "If grace abounds so freely, is it okay for us to abandon restraint and sin ourselves silly?" The answer to such a senseless question should be obvious. Why on earth would we misuse the very grace that saved us from self-destructive muck, to return to it? [115]

When we are really desperate, we may even resort to begging God. But begging is not going to get us anywhere with Him. He deals with us according to covenant. Covenant is a binding agreement that obliges the parties to the covenant to carry out what has been agreed upon. When we get to know our covenant privileges, the need for begging ceases. So much of what we beg for has already been decided upon in the covenant—it's entirely ours. When we understand our covenant privileges, our prayers take on an air of confidence.

Tradition would have us believe that the parable Jesus told about nagging for bread from a friend in the middle of the night, illustrates that we are expected to repeatedly beg God until He reluctantly gives in to our tiresome pestering[98]. We must irritate Him sufficiently before He grudgingly grants us our request. Like the man in this story, God eventually gives in just to get us off His back. If that's what we have come to believe, then we would have to conclude that God is unwilling to bless us, and that He sees us as an irksome nuisance. This view is simply not consistent with the God of the Bible—quite obviously the metaphor is misunderstood.

The question to ask oneself is, "Who am I in this story? Am I the beggar, or am I the child tucked up snugly in bed at home with dad?" No doubt, the child went to bed on a full stomach, and you can be quite sure that the child did not have to beg for supper. Thank God we are not beggars; we are children, and that makes all the difference. David said, "I have never seen the godly forsaken, nor their children begging for bread".[111]

Jesus said that at the precise moment of prayer, we should be entirely convinced that we have received the answer to our prayer, even though the answer may not immediately be evident[10]. Praying a second time would be tantamount to admitting that we did not receive by faith at the precise moment of our first prayer. Each subsequent prayer simply confirms our doubts, thus cancelling previous prayers.

That being the case, why would we find it necessary to nag God? Sure, there should be subsequent prayer, but unless such prayers support our initial request, they serve only to demonstrate unbelief. Giving thanks, on the other hand, is an expression of unflinching confidence—transforming desperation into gratitude! Faith is not about begging for hand-outs; it's about confident expectation. It's not about hoping; it's about knowing!

This comment is not meant to be just another religious formula. After Jesus had spat in the blind man's eyes, his eyesight was only partially restored. It was only after a subsequent touch from Jesus that his sight was fully restored[112]. Jesus made a habit of breaking religious formulas and so should we—not for the sake of breaking them, but for the sake of being Spirit led.

When I worked at a bank, "customer covenant" was what was agreed upon between a bank relationship manager and his client. Basically, the bank makes a promise to honour all cheques up to an agreed upon overdraft limit, and the client promises not to exceed that limit. Provided cheques are within the agreed limit, the bank has no right to dishonour them. The terms of this covenant agreement are decided upon in advance, way before any cheques are written. At the time of the agreement, the bank has no idea of what cheques will be presented for payment, and therefore cannot refuse to honour them—it is bound by covenant!

God decided on the terms of the covenant, but mankind was incapable of meeting the required level of performance, so the son of man, Jesus Himself, was given power of attorney to agree upon the terms of the covenant with God on mankind's behalf. Then He did the unthinkable. In one fell swoop, He fulfilled the entire covenant on behalf of mankind, validating it with a signature signed in blood. This made the covenant agreement binding on both parties, i.e. both God and man. In this agreement, the limits and responsibilities of the parties were agreed upon in advance. The limit that God agreed to was infinity—He is willing and able to do way in excess of our most outrages requests[85]. He has agreed that the blood of Jesus is sufficient payment for the record of our sins to be expunged from the record books of heaven, and that no further recording of our sins be permitted[82]. In heaven's chronicles, it is as though we have never committed a single sin[66].

Seeing that our side of the covenant has been fulfilled in full by our divine representative, Jesus, we have every right to expect God the Father to fulfil His side of the deal. He expects nothing from us except childlike faith. When it is by grace, it is entirely free and undeserved.

He has agreed:

- that the blood that Jesus shed on the cross for us is enough to wash away our sins[110].
- that the stripes that Jesus suffered at the hands of the Roman soldier is sufficient payment to facilitate our healing[6].
- that the poverty that Jesus experienced is sufficient payment to facilitate our prosperity[7].
- that we have power of attorney to use the name of Jesus to ask the Father for anything and it will be given[8].
- that if we knock on God's door, it will be opened to us[9].
- that if we seek for God's answers, He will answer[9].
- that we can have whatever we ask for provided we actually believe that we have received it before it materialises[10].
- that we can have whatever we say, as long as our words are accompanied by faith[11].
- that whatever we bind on earth will be bound in heaven, and whatever we loose on earth will be loosed in heaven[12].
- that we can lay claim to any promise He has made to us.
- that He would multiply what we sow[4].

What an amazing covenant! And to make absolutely sure that we do not mistake it for an obligation to perform for God, He sealed it in a Last Will and Testament. As with all Testaments, beneficiaries are at liberty to claim the assets bequeathed to them without payment. Assets are not automatically dispersed to beneficiaries; they must be claimed. For this, faith is required. Without faith, blood bought rights remain unclaimed and unused. In order to understand grace, we must make it our business to know what has been bequeathed to us. Our rights and privileges are clearly stated in the Testament, and thankfully, they come without strings attached.

In truth, Jesus, the son of man, has already fulfilled mankind's side of the deal, thereby obligating the other party to the covenant, i.e. God the Father, to fulfil His side—something He does with aplomb! Thankfully, everything that needs to be done, has been done. For example, when we pray for healing, God doesn't have to lift a finger[6].

From His side, it's all done and dusted—there is no need to send Jesus back to the Roman soldier for more whipping to obtain more healing for us. When Jesus said, "It is finished", He really meant every word He said[13]. All the healing that you will ever need was made available to you—He did it before you were born¬, long before you could make some kind of contribution to deserve it. His covenant with you is all about pure unadulterated, undeserved and undiluted gratuitous favour—don't make the mistake of watering it down by attempting to curry favour with God.

"Does that mean that I can be disobedient with impunity?" It no longer surprises me to have this question pop up whenever grace is mentioned. It was the same for Paul. Let's be realistic; who are we more likely to obey? A tough task master who rules with punitive laws or the Lover of our souls who lavishes affection upon us? In reality, grace does not inspire sin; it inspires obedience at a level that can only be understood by believers who walk by grace. Sadly, all too often, believers allow their religious legacies to convince them that grace is tantamount to rebellion.

The next question that pops up from grace sceptics is, "If all of this is by grace, then does grace make good works bad?" Really! I mean really! Sceptics just don't seem to get it! The love we get becomes the love we redistribute to those around us. Surely it is obvious? Good works have no inherent value, unless done with grace!

OLDER BROTHER MENTALITY

As early as I can remember as a child, Christianity was about rules and discipline. Sunday was a day of rest. My mother couldn't even sew on that day. It would be like, "Sticking a needle into Jesus' eye", she would say. In the Orange Free State Province, fishing, that most restful of all pastimes, was legislatively outlawed on Sundays for religious reasons. Anyone daring to defy the Province's Sabbath Law had to answer to the courts. In legalistic church circles, women were drab and unattractive—they couldn't wear make-up and their hair could not be dyed. They were not allowed to wear slacks, certainly not shorts. Neither men nor women wore denim jeans. Women's hair had to be long, and men's had to be short. Many women wore their hair in a bun, and men had military regulation short back and sides haircuts. You wore a suit to church—you had to look the part and be at your "Sunday best".

I was not allowed to go to the movies, and as a result, I could not participate in school boy discussions about the wonderful Westerns of that era. When I was older, I sneaked out to bioscope anyway. I was not allowed to go to dances, so I never got to know the girls who did. When my father bought me a saxophone, I had to promise that I would never play it in a dance band. I was not allowed to smoke, so I did it secretly.

In the early seventies, my sister visited a church after not having attended church for ten years. As a hippie, her style of clothing was somewhat unconventional—very different to the formal church attire of that era. Instead of a warm welcome home, she was made to feel decidedly uncomfortable as she listened to the undercurrents of a sermon that was quite obviously aimed to shame her for her inappropriate attire in church. This was the best welcome that the pastor could dream up for a prodigal daughter who had come home after a long godless sojourn in a far country. Her hippie style of dress did not measure up to religion's snobbery. This was a suit and hat wearing, ten-pound King James Bible-carrying church. After such a cold shoulder encounter, it would be perfectly understandable if she never to set foot in a church again.

She knew a biker guy in her street who was always high on drugs; so much so that he earned himself the nickname of "Joe Make-a-Blow". When she heard that he had become a "happy clappy believer", she decided to pay him a visit. He wasn't home, but as she was turning to leave, he arrived with a carload of young hippie believers. When she told him that she had become a believer, he was so overjoyed that he threw his arms around her and spun her around, while the carload of hippie new believers joyously shrieked their delight!

Although God the Father hadn't appeared to my sister in person to express His joy at her home coming, He dispatched a minister of the gospel to do it for Him. Sadly, the minister botched his assignment. No problem for God—He swung plan B into action—He dispatched a raggedy carload of scruffy drug addicts to represent Him. Fortunately, they did a decidedly better job of revealing His pleasure and delight at having His beloved prodigal daughter home.

Religion's bungling best could not reveal God's heart to her, instead it did a fine job of trashing His fine character. A bedraggled bunch of misfits did a decidedly better job of it. The loving heart of God—His sheer joy and complete acceptance of my sister in her bedraggled state, shone through a bunch of outcasts that fine day. Their welcome home was distinctly warmer than the cold shoulder treatment of prim and proper churchies.

Her church "welcome" was very different to the story that Jesus told of the prodigal son's return after his long hedonistic sojourn in a foreign land[14]. His father didn't even wait for him to change out of his filthy clothes—he didn't even give him an opportunity to beg for forgiveness—He was too busy kissing him all over his sweaty face and neck, totally unconcerned that he was contaminating himself with a mingled stench of pig swill and body odour. He was so overwhelmed with his son's homecoming that his shabby attire went by unnoticed.

The prodigal's older brother didn't share his father's delight, choosing rather to be offended by his father's extravagant display of emotion for a scallywag. In the same way, not every modern-day church elder has sympathy for saintly offenders. They would sooner point an accusing finger in their faces than put a kiss on their cheeks. They forget that Jesus had no problem dealing with misfits—he was happy to associate with the dregs of society, and happy for the spiritual elite to know it. Yes, we often see modern-day offenders welcomed home, but very often their welcome comes with conditions. While they are being lectured by the sanctimonious for their indiscretions, you can be quite sure that our heavenly Father is giving them the red-carpet treatment!

Imagine how different the welcome would have been had the older brother been the first to see the prodigal arrive home. No doubt, the prodigal would have turned away in sheer disappointment; never coming to discover his father's complete acceptance and forgiveness.

Often offenders are required to submit to a process of remorse, repentance, discipline, discipleship and to show fruits of repentance before any notion of reinstatement can be considered. Like the older brother, the snobbish pastor would have been awfully offended if he had found out that my sister's heavenly Father had dispatched a motely bunch of dropouts to welcome her home.

While the minister was expecting apologies from a contrite heart, our heavenly Father was hushing her, telling her that no words of self-recrimination were necessary—no apologies required. He didn't expect any cowering; it was a time for embracing, celebrating, laughter, rejoicing, dancing and whooping!

The older brother in this story is a picture of the sanctimonious faithful of our day. Their holier than thou demeanour says it all. Sadly, it is older brother mentality that gives Christianity a bad name. A judgemental mentality just cannot come to terms with a concept that forgives as readily as the prodigal's father.

Prejudice and judgemental attitudes have got to be the least attractive traits in a believer. Conversely, an attitude of mercy and grace is usually so unexpected that it dismantles the sturdiest of barriers and wins friends without even trying. Mercy carries within itself the power to melt the stoniest of hearts. Animosity crumbles when confronted with outright forgiveness; it cannot withstand the power of undeserved love—grace carries far more influence than the most pious of accusations.

The prodigal's older brother felt that he only got his father's approval when he had done something to deserve it. How could this low-life have gotten such special treatment, especially considering the damage he had brought upon the family name? What was there to celebrate? He felt that his father was wasting his affection on somebody who would just as likely let him down again as before. In his estimation, the prodigal was nothing more than a vagabond who had squandered the family fortune and dragged their respected family name through the mud. For the life of him, he could not think of a single thing worthy of his father's affection.

Intimacy with our heavenly Father is not something that people with "older brother mentality" can understand, leave alone indulge in. The depth of depravity and wantonness to which the prodigal had sunk, gave him greater insight into how gracious his father actually was. The older brother's self-righteousness prevented him from making this discovery—his would remain a superficial relationship. The depth of our heavenly Father's love is only truly known by those who have experienced His loving embrace while still in a state of bedragglement. Actually, we are all in a scruffy state, but religion has convinced us to pretend that we are not.

Like the older brother, religion puts distance into romance—it is too stiff for such soppiness.

The reason that the younger son became a prodigal in the first place, was in all likelihood because of the older brother's holier than thou attitude. This kind of sanctimonious superiority is enough to drive the sincerest of followers away. Very often, in religion's quest to produce disciples, it only succeeds in cloning older brothers. It's this mentality that leads to the disillusionment of so many seekers. They may see through the pretence of it all, and become prodigals themselves. Older brothers have earned their places of honour in the congregation, but sadly, this kind of mentality keeps them from indulging in the delights of grace.

Religion says that favour follows repentance, but the Bible tells a different story—it says that repentance follows favour[15]. The sequence may not seem important, but it has a vastly different outcome. In the parable of the prodigal son, the son didn't even get to express an apology. His only act of repentance was to return home. The father had been waiting with his mind already made up to forgive him. We are forgiven in advance at the cross. All that is left for us to do is to pitch up and soak up Dad's love. What starts out in repentance and sorrow, soon turns into merriment and celebration.

Love has the power to bring about genuine change. Why? Because love has a way of stealing our hearts. Legalism cannot achieve this. How can it? It attempts to deal with surface matters—the superficiality of behaviour. But hearts cannot be changed from the outside; they can only be changed from within, and it takes love to do that! The older brother had the credentials and an impeccable record to match, but his heart had not been transformed by his father's loving touch—such soppiness is beneath the dignity of self-assured and self-made men.

The older brother's self-righteousness had prevented him from discovering how deeply his father loved him. Oh how magnificent it is to be defective—if we weren't, how would we ever know the height, depth, length and width of God's love for us? Jesus said that he who has been forgiven much, loves much[16]. But religion is different! It puts holiness before love and grace. And that, more than anything else, leads to shallow holiness! Before one knows it, one is contriving an unholy form of holiness for the sake of fitting in. Let's be honest, contrived holiness is a country mile from genuine holiness! And our best attempts at holiness are nothing other than engineered holiness—God calls it "filth rags"!

Often we can be awfully harsh on ourselves—examining our motives for returning to God. Let's not kid ourselves, the prodigal's motives for returning home were not necessarily noble—he returned, because the moment his money ran out, his fair-weather friends deserted him like rats fleeing a sinking ship. When he could no longer afford to buy the rounds, they had no further reason to admire him.

When the "high life" of wine, woman and song petered out, he was reduced to scrounging for filthy meals of husks salvaged from the pig slop. Racked with hunger pangs, desperate for a decent meal, he made his way home in the hope of getting a job on his father's farm. It wasn't that his heart was moved by something as pure as affection for his dad—he was clutching at straws—desperate to stay alive!

If our motives for wanting God back in our lives are less than perfect, God does not even flinch, He is delighted to have us back. Relax—He is not offended by our lack of perfection—He is gracious enough to look past our self-centeredness.

On the prodigal's arrival home, his misdemeanours and shallow motives went by unnoticed. He was expecting a telling-off from his father, but it never came. His father knew that a tongue lashing would not touch his heart in the way that a lavishing of unconditional love would. It took this kind of love and acceptance to touch his battered and bruised heart. Nothing less than unconditional love could turn disillusionment and disappointment into value and worth. Nothing less than unconditional love could tenderise the hard calluses seared into his once tender heart—a heart injured by self-recrimination and shame. Nothing but pure undeserved love could arrest his heart and influence his values and outlook on life. Nothing but loving grace could cause him to turn his back on a prodigal lifestyle. Nothing less than unmerited love could restore his faith in his family.

Before we even begin to plead for mercy, we are already accepted. Clemency has already been decided upon, ready and waiting to be appropriated. We don't have to persuade God to pardon us—He is delighted to do so. Only God can make forgiveness a celebration. He doesn't expect us to grovel, He doesn't make us feel like we are bothering Him, He just wants us to absorb His fatherly love and know that all is forgiven. We are entirely understood and immensely appreciated.

What could be more convincing of God's unconditional love than the actions of a father who recognised the familiar gait of his son while still a long way off. He didn't wait to see how contrite and sorry his son was before considering whether or not he deserved forgiveness. Abandoning all dignity and decorum, he lifted his skirts and ran towards his son, threw his arms around him and kissed him extravagantly and unashamedly.

Although the son had prepared a speech of repentance, his father would hear nothing of it for the sheer joy of having him back home. He had no lecture for his son; no words of recrimination or blame; no "I could have told you so" speeches; no demands for explanations or apologies. His dad simply received him back without even so much as asking him to promise never to do it again.

Our heavenly Father just wants us to pitch up—He doesn't expect us to be all cut up and sorry. He is not looking for perfection in us, not even the slightest hint of anything commendable in us before deciding whether or not to welcome us home. He does not call for wallowing in remorse, contrition and self-condemnation. He knows that we will still secretly miss, and possibly even long for the very things that we have left behind, but He embraces and kisses us all the same.

We may have come back simply because we couldn't make it on our own. Even so, God's old oak tree is laden with yellow ribbons, and every one of them screams out God's unconditional welcome home!

"Come on home—no explanations needed!"

FREAKISH RELIGION

On our first honeymoon night, hotel management graciously sent a complimentary bottle of Champagne to our room. We ungraciously sent it straight back—we were too religious for that. How noble we were! On second thoughts—how nauseating we were!

Looking back, we were a peculiar bunch of freaks. But we weren't fazed by that label. We were taught that the Bible expected us to be a "peculiar people". Unfortunately, we took that to mean outward peculiarity. To us, the label of "weirdoes" was not an insult; it was a compliment! It validated our Christian stand. But what we didn't understand was that God had something quite different in mind when he defined us as peculiar; something very foreign to our legalistically steeped minds. It was inward peculiarity. The problem with outward peculiarity was that our hearts could stay dark, and this darkness could be masked with a contrived appearance of "saintliness". Although ugly is certainly not saintly, we had our own weird ideas about godliness. Looking back, I have to admit, our behaviour was bizarre to say the least!

My childhood friend's father was a pious and friendly man, well liked and highly respected as a saintly church leader. Nobody could ever have imagined the darkness lurking in his heart. Like the rest of us, he was adept at hiding his true feelings.

I was sleeping over at his home on the night of the church's annual general meeting. The congregation did not re-elect him onto the church board. That night at church, he took the news graciously as one would expect from such a courteous man, but the moment he got home, he vented his feelings in the most appalling of ways. Before he let rip, his children sensed what was coming and scattered. Anything he could lay his hands on became a projectile, and anything that got in his way was booted aside in anger as he broadcasted his outrage with words that he wouldn't dare use in church.

Regretfully, legalistic holiness does not deal with the heart, it deals with outward appearances—it has no remedies for the evil seated in our hearts. Inner darkness remains unchallenged—allowed to fester in secret.

Only God's unmerited love is able to bypass our shame and reach all the way down into the depths of our being without the slightest regard for our state of bedragglement. Legalism tries to change our bedraggled behaviour, but it has no answers for the attitudes of our hearts. It takes love to challenge attitudes, and unchallenged attitudes produce questionable behaviour.

Christians, in this day and age, are a lot more relaxed about draconian legalistic codes, but these codes have not disappeared, they persist in a different guise. We have simply exchanged the old list for a new list of do's and don'ts.

Authentic Christianity does not need do's and don'ts to accomplish upright living. Whether we live by these codes or not, we are all loved regardless. The discovery of how deeply we are loved is heart enthralling stuff. Without consciously trying, we find ourselves responding to people and circumstances with less irritation. Somehow we find that we have patience for the most annoying of irksome individuals—they no longer exasperate us. You don't have to be a psychologist to know that loved people love people! And that goes for loving God too! It takes a special kind of unqualified love to win our affections, and God has plenty to give. Although grace does not dictate behaviour, behaviour responds well to love, and it does so without effort.

When we are judged, we become defensive, preventing accusers from reaching our soft sides; but when we are loved, we feel safe enough to drop our defences and allow people into the secret places of our hearts. When you accept me as I am, I no longer need to prove myself—there is no need to impress you with my saintly pedigree or with my King Solomon like wisdom—no need for posturing and name dropping. I feel safe to be vulnerable with you—your love opens the way for me to be honest and transparent.

When we come to realise how unaffected God's love is by anything that we have done or not done, and how infinitely accepted we are in our present less than perfect condition, something within us softens and lets Him into our secret places. Our fears for tomorrow fade and a confidence arises on the inside. All of this takes place when His love dispels our fears[63].

In charismatic churches, we can mask the darkness of our souls and appear pious by smiling, raising our hands in worship, clapping to the rhythm of the songs, doing the charismatic jig, and chorusing our amens when appropriate. In traditional churches we can mask the darkness of our souls and appear pious by quietly listening to the sermon, singing along with the congregation and following the order of service. When it is all about outward appearances, what's going on within can remain secret.

Although legalism has much to say about appearances, it has no answers for what's going on in our hearts. Grace, on the other hand, requires no laws—God's love changes our hearts and changed hearts have different aspirations. It leads to unforced behavioural changes that come about without conscious effort. Grace is the answer to the Christian malady commonly known as "hypocrisy".

Despite our most determined resolve, we simply cannot change ourselves inwardly—a task beyond the capability of humanity. So we settle for pretence. At least, by feigning holiness, we stand a chance of gaining the approval of our peers. Feigning holiness is not a problem for religious people—it is quite acceptable when everybody else is also pretending.

Religion's way of using God's wrath to frighten us into changing may achieve temporary change, but the terror of it soon fades. Subsequent doses of fear are needed to keep the scary fires aflame. We must be kept running scared enough to meet with religion's "holy" expectations. Conversely, the value that we receive from being unconditionally loved has a way of changing our inherent way of thinking. Being loved in such a complete way is profoundly influential upon the direction our lives take—change follows without effort.

Instead of finger pointing, blaming and reprimanding, God's way of shaping our behaviour involves nothing more than grace. When we discover that we are loved despite our shabbiness, and not even expected to make any promises to change, our resistance melts, and we find it easy to make room for whatever God desires of us.

PROBLEMS AND PERSPECTIVES

Legalism, religion's twin brother, paints a utopian picture of life without sin. But unachievable ideals are dangerous. Failure is inevitable, and each failure chips away at our faith until we are left with nothing but a sense of defeat, the perfect environment for the incubation of religious flakiness.

Legalists are quick to point out that John, in his first letter stated that Christians do not sin[99]. On the surface, this statement brings everybody's salvation into question, because quite frankly, everybody sins. Legalists get around this conundrum by saying that sin comes in different forms: there is deliberate sin and there is normal sin. The problem with that kind of thinking is that the Bible makes no such distinction—sin is sin—if we are guilty of one, we are guilty of all. Besides, all believers sin deliberately. When we break the speed limit, we are doing it on purpose—when we bicker, we are doing it on purpose.

If John was making a point for legalism, then every single Christian is in big trouble. But is that really what he was saying? John was well aware that we all sin—he said as much in the same letter. He pulled no punches when He said that we would be lying if we said that we have no sin, and then went on to tell us what to do when we sin. Not only that, he also told us what Jesus would do on our behalf[100].

Legalists will counter this argument with David's words that God would not hear him if he regarded iniquity in his heart[107]. But when Adam and Eve sinned, God did not turn from them—He came looking for them! He saw no reason to end their relationship[108]. In reality, it was not God who had left them; it was them who had left God. Why did they run? Because of shame—a self-defeating condition seriously detrimental to any relationship!

Although we will never stop sinning this side of heaven, the whole sin issue has been dealt with on the cross[66]. It's the embarrassment—our shame that separates us. Although we are forgiven in advance at the cross, we only come to experience the fullness of it to the degree that we find it in our hearts to forgive ourselves and others[109].

New Christians set out excitedly with their newfound gift of righteousness, only to come to the disappointing realisation that they have not stopped sinning. From a legalistic standpoint, they are not making it, and this leaves them with a sense of disillusionment. And that's not where it ends. Faking it becomes their only option. Legalism can set a person off on an impossible mission. Failure to meet unrealistic standards is inevitable, and before we know it, our faith is clouded with a sense of unworthiness.

In reality, Christians continue to sin[33] and God is not uncomfortable with this. He knows that we are better off without sin, but He is realistic—He is well aware that sinlessness is beyond the capacity of mankind. Our righteous status was not awarded to us for behaving well; it was awarded to us for believing well—it's purely a matter of faith[102].

Have you noticed how satisfying it is for unbelievers to discover that Christian's continue to sin—it makes for juicy gossip, doesn't it? But then again, when Christians insist on acting out their holier than thou charades, who can blame unbelievers for coming to these unfortunate conclusions.

"No thank you, we don't do this or that" we may say with disdain, or "You are blaspheming my best Friend". If Christians insist on belittling non-Christians, who can blame them for responding with cynicism? Does God want to straighten out their language, or does He want them to surrender their hearts to Him? After all, don't surrendered hearts speak a different language? One thing is certain; going out of our way to belittle unbelievers in this way does not go very far towards winning friends and influencing people to receive Jesus into their lives.

As Christians, we unashamedly nail our colours to the mast and make no apologies for our stand—an honour to stand up and be counted for Jesus! We have the light of God's life within us, but often allow a critical spirit to blur the light we emit to those around us. People respond positively to our love, and negatively to our religious criticism. The problem with criticism is that it shines a very irksome light. On the other hand, graciousness gives others what they don't deserve. The light that grace shines, gives honour and understanding to the most disagreeable of characters. With grace they are drawn to the Christ within us like moths drawn to a streetlamp. When people are accepted exactly as they are, without being expected to conform to anything, you can be sure that they will return for more. It is not our words that leave a lasting impression; it is how we make people feel! And nobody can edify a person like Jesus within us!

My late brother-in-law was one such individual. He had a way of making anybody he met feel special. What a precious gift! In a matter of days, without a single word of instruction from him, his gracious ways taught me more about the true meaning of grace than twenty years of sermons. What is it that is so special about grace? To put it plainly, it gives honour where honour is not due! Nothing can be more edifying—it brings out the very best from the very worst of us! My brother-in-law had me coming back for more, time and again. Sadly for us, he went on to be with his Lord. But fortunately, he left us with something immensely precious—his legacy of graciousness lives on in the countless lives he touched.

Sadly, the same cannot be said for people encumbered by legalism—they have little forbearance when encountering irksome in others—seeing it as their divine duty to confront sin wherever they see it. They are easily offended by fellow believers who have found liberty in Jesus. Although unlikely to admit it, their priorities are obvious—for them "sin centricity" outranks "soul centricity"! Correcting offenders, rather than making room in their hearts to love and accept them exactly as they are. People are looking for answers to life's harsh treatment. But they are unlikely to come to us for help when all they get from us is criticism. Unless we love them just as they are, how will they ever get to see Jesus in us?

There is no question about it, all Christians continue sinning until the day they die—John is clear on this[33]. It seems like an oxymoron doesn't it? Although God sees us as sinless; yet we cannot deny that we still sin[101].

Unfortunately, those who deny their sinfulness, end up living double lives—always giving the appearance of Mr or Mrs perfect Christian, seldom admitting to having secrets, like bottled up anger and improper fantasies. Admitting to their weaknesses would be tantamount to admitting that they have failed the test of authenticity—or so they think.

Transparency and vulnerability are just not possible when religious expectations run high—each one feels the need to show a life that is unblemished and perfect in every way. But nothing could be more false and flaky than keeping up appearances with the saintly Jones'. The fact that other Christians are doing the same does not make pious charading any more honest.

In our early years of marriage, without the church saying it in so many words, we nevertheless felt religiously obliged to keep up the appearance of a perfect Christian family. Every other religious family appeared to be perfect. Unfortunately, this led me to be overbearing and controlling. I could not risk Susan being honest about us, so would often interrupt her conversations to rescue her from the possibility of exposing our real lives to fellow Christians. The faith that we were professing always had to appear flawless to our Christian compatriots. No doubt, we were not impressing anybody; they were playing the same flaky game with us. Hypocrisy had consigned our inter-personal relationships to shallowness! Besides striving to be seen to be a perfect Christian family, we also felt religiously compelled to give the appearance of divine prosperity and divine health. What frauds we were!

One of our friends was particularly domineering. He kept a tight rein on his family, often resorting to anger to manipulate and control. When eventually his children flew the coop, it was not surprising to hear that they were experimenting with all that the world had to offer. Control is an evil akin to witchcraft, and precisely opposite to grace.

Children are likely to relate to their heavenly Father in the same way they related to their earthly fathers. In a family where love is dispensed in proportion to obedience, the concept of being loved without regard for obedience is unlikely to be understood. To them, grace will remain a mystery.

While not necessarily broadcast over the church's PA, nevertheless church members can be excused for feeling a surreptitious pressure to conform to the unspoken expectations of their particular congregation. Wherever religious expectations are encountered, charading is encountered—it comes with the territory! On the surface, all must appear to be going swimmingly, even though our world may be crumbling around our feet. Although hurting on the inside, nobody must be allowed to discover that we are less than the image we are portraying. Although desperately needing help from compatriots, how could we possibly confide in the very people we are trying to impress?

Is there an answer to this shallowness? Thankfully yes! In a word, it is grace! When we discover that, even though we are far from perfect, we are nevertheless truly loved, a healthy self-love develops. When we have self-esteem, we have no need to seek validation from public approval.

When we realise that, despite our tardy state, we are nevertheless unconditionally loved, it throws a whole new light on everything. We find hope in the face of despair. With God's smile upon us, optimism comes easily. And faith thrives on optimism!

There is another religious misgiving. So often people are led to believe that when they become Christians, all their problems go away. Bur whether we are prepared to admit it or not, problems remain a factor in every Christian's life. The difference for Christians is that God has promised to deliver us out of all of them[51].

A modern-day Good Samaritan was waiting for the arrival of a flight when he noticed a weary traveller who seemed to be carrying the weight of the world on his shoulders. Gloom written all over his face, feet dragging, head bowed, shoulders sagging; quite obviously weighed down by life's unfair twists and turns. The Samaritan was moved to somehow lend a helping hand—but how could he help this weary stranger without offending him?

An analytical person would probably want to know what the underlying cause was before offering a solution; but sharing his heart with a stranger would be most unlikely. An amiable person would probably want to give him a shoulder to cry on; but intimacy with a stranger would be just as unlikely. An expressive person would in all likelihood try to make him laugh; but after a brief moment of comic relief, he would be left to face the same problems. An assertive personality would almost certainly sternly tell him to snap out of it; but snapping out of it does not solve the underlying problem. A psychologist may ask him to verbalise his despair; but he would sooner run away from his problems than admit to them. A pastor may want to pray with him; but he may not necessarily be ready to see prayer as a solution.

None of these strategies could have done as much for the weary traveller as what the Samaritan did for him that day. He walked up behind the man, tapped him on the shoulder and said, "Excuse me sir, God loves you and so do I". The man's demeanour visibly changed before his eyes—he immediately straightened up, put his shoulders back and walked away with a bounce to his stride.

A timely word from God can bring about a new perspective to life. Towering mountains become mere mole hills, and what seemed impossible is gloriously possible. It's not that the problem diminishes; it's the vantage point from which the problem is viewed that changes. From a different angle it loses its ominousness. A lofty mountain looks insignificant from the vantage point of a jet airliner at cruising altitude. Same mountain; yet decidedly less intimidating!

When problems are seen as opportunities, they lose their power to frighten us. Most of the world's greatest inventions were born out of desperate necessity and seemingly insurmountable obstacles. As they say in the classics, "Necessity is the father of invention". Simple modern-day conveniences are ours purely because somebody tenaciously tackled problems, using one obstacle after another as stepping stones to come up with inventions that make life easier for us all.

Everything has been put under Jesus' feet[50], so when we discover that we are the body of Christ, we no longer look up to find problems towering over us, we look down from the vantage point of His body and find them under our feet. No matter how daunting our problems may appear, when we see that they are under His feet and therefore under our feet, they lose their ominousness. From this vantage point, we are able to think more clearly and apply our minds and faith to problems that would otherwise crush us.

God has not left us to strive for victory; the enemy is already defeated; the battle is over—we simply enforce the victory that Jesus won on the cross—ours for the taking. With grace, everything takes on a different perspective! A super glorious perspective!

GRACE REJECTED

I count myself privileged to have been involved in a wonderful spiritual awakening. In the 1980s our tiny congregation multiplied tenfold overnight. We were bursting at the seams—if you didn't have a seat by half an hour before start of service, you were out of luck. Aisles, stage and foyer would be fully occupied by then. Even standing room would be taken.

This raging wildfire burnt brightly for about five years. Sadly, it was smothered out when the tone of the service changed from grace to legalism. One of the church board members stated that the church had become a freight train without breaks. He said that while our new believers understood spiritual matters, they did not understand the moral code of Christian living. Our preacher was urged to change his emphasis. That was the beginning of the end of something extraordinarily beautiful.

Later, in a desperate bid to rekindle the fire, instead of turning to grace, they turned to even more draconian levels of legalism. They introduced a document entitled "The Spiritual and Moral Qualifications for Church Membership". It contained a legalistic list of do's and don'ts. Every member was required to endorse the document to affirm their commitment to it. Instead of purifying the congregation, the last glowing embers of a once rampant revival fire was finally and permanently extinguished. To this day, empty pews bear witness to the emptiness of legalism. Those who participated in this revival have first-hand evidence that the Spirit of God moves in an environment of freedom—the kind of freedom that incubates in the liberty of grace. But the freedom of grace can seem frightening when viewed from the pavilions of legalism. Religion simply cannot come to terms with the liberty and freedom that comes with grace. In religion's estimation, grace is far too un-legalistic and relaxed to be religious. How sad it is for those, who in the interests of holiness, fail to appreciate that holiness is only holy when it is a product of the free flowing rhythms of grace. They cannot grasp the fact that grace is God's idea, and that sanctification by any other means is blatant fraudulence!

> Goosey Goosey Gander where shall I wander,
> Upstairs, downstairs and in my lady's chamber,
> There I met an old man who wouldn't say his prayers,
> I took him by the left leg and threw him down the stairs.

If you want proof that religion does not understand grace, look no further. This sixteenth century nursery rhyme bears historical testimony to religion's appalling record of prejudice and intolerance.

Catholic priests would hide in "Priest Holes" (very small secret rooms once found in many great houses in England) to avoid persecution from zealous Protestants who were strong opponents of Catholicism. If caught, both the priest and all the members of the family found harbouring him were summarily executed. The moral in Goosey Goosey Gander's lyrics implied that something rather unpleasant like death would surely be pronounced upon anyone failing to say their prayers correctly—meaning prays said in English, which was the Protestant way, as opposed to Latin, which was the Catholic way!

This is an obvious example of religion gone berserk. Modern day examples may be less obvious, but just as ungracious and equally out of character with a God of love. Seeing we all read the same Bible and worship the same God, why in the world are we at odds with each other? How is it possible that Christian denominations quarrel over finer points of theology? How in the world did this kind of disunity enter a kingdom that should be characterised by unity, forgiveness and love? Let's face it, Christianity at odds with Christianity, is a kingdom divided against itself. Surely bickering and backbiting belong to another kingdom—a shameful kingdom, where destroying each other is normal? Yet whole sermons are regularly expounded from pulpits discrediting the grace that not only saved them but keeps them saved. How is it possible that respected clergymen have the courage to undermine the very fundamental of fundamentals of our faith?

I witnessed to the Buddhist Chinese gentleman who runs our favourite sushi restaurant. He clearly pointed out that if he were to accept Christianity, his faith would immediately be challenged by countless Christian denominations wrestling for religious dominance. From the outside looking in, all he could see was a religion intent on destroying itself—something that most Christians have come to terms with. But, religious rivalry is so far removed from anything remotely Christian, that it borders on un-Christian!

If there is only one truth, then the fact that there are a thousand denominations tells us that there are at least a thousand religious errors. The truth is: God is not in the least bit bothered with the accuracy of our interpretations, or with the correctness of our procedures and ceremonies—He is interested in our friendship!

We see new denominations popping up like popcorn in a hot pot without a lid. Factions within factions feeling strongly enough about some finer point of interpretation—reason enough to hive off and start a new school of thought. Tragically, there are some who desert a denomination to form a new one simply because they could not get their way.

Often the clergy reserves the exclusive right to discover and disseminate God's revelations. Little regard is given to contributions from congregants. Only paradigms that run true to denominational dogma are allowed to be publicly expressed. Blind submission to the ideas of the leader is expected.

This hard-line may seem noble to some, but what is the good of it if it robs people of the privilege of hearing God for themselves? When we exchange an intimate romance with the King for an arm's length arrangement via the clergy, what are we left with? Nothing but empty religious nonsense! Isn't this the very thing from which Jesus rescued us?

The clergy may know a lot, but the truth is that nobody has a complete picture of God's love—that's because He hasn't finished revealing how gracious He really is. Paul said that discovering His love is a continuous quest—the depths of which will never be fully known[17].

Many are convinced that they know how far God's grace extends, and have come to reject any suggestion that it could exceed the boundaries they have set. But should we really be squeezing God's love into denominational boxes? His love is immeasurable—way beyond our wildest imaginations—beyond the boundaries set by any denomination. So enormous that not even the saintly Paul could come to grips with it[137]!

When it comes to religious conformity, you cannot expect grace junkies to fit in—the very essence of grace does not allow for conformity, so it is perfectly natural for grace junkies to stick out like sore thumbs! These are believers who prize the value they have gained from God's love—trouncing the need to be religiously admired. Even if they must be despised, what is the value of respect if it comes at the expense of the glory of knowing the depths of God's love? The enthrallment of His love is something that cannot be understood by religious folk. For grace junkies, there is no holding back—they are prepared to walk on water, if that is what it will take to know Him more intimately. Once a person has gotten high on God's love, it is too late for religion to rein them in—to them, religion is a lost cause. They have discovered that holiness cannot be achieved with religious restraints; it can only be achieved by the grace granted by God for this purpose. Their hearts have been captivated—enthralled by the continuous unfolding of fresh insights into the depth of His love for them. They can hardly wait for their next rendezvous with Jesus.

"He loves me! He loves me! He loves me! I don't understand why, but thankfully, He does!"

Religious brainwashing is not God's idea—He grants us freedom of choice. The Bible warns us against manipulation. It is nothing short of bewitchment. It is as much a religious problem in our day and age as it was in Paul's, and he spared no words in stressing the dangers of this dastardly un-Christlike practice. Religious control stifles an individual's personal search for God's ways, and runs contrary to Jesus' commandment for all believers to seek the kingdom for themselves[97].

I heard a sermon from an associate pastor who continuously, in a subservient way, assured the congregation that the points he was making were views shared by their senior pastor. I imagine that such deference becomes necessary when all revelation must come via the "top dog"—no room is left for personal revelation.

I once asked a pastor of a large congregation how he managed to hear from the Lord for each and every sermon. His answer took me by surprise. He said, "Deon, it's scary out there! Often there is no leading—it becomes a case of conjuring up something from the distant past, or just being plain creative." Are we placing more credence upon what is said from the pulpit, than upon the still small voice of the Spirit?

Of all the revelation that we acquire, how much of it comes to us through our personal connection with God, and how much via the pulpit? If our answer is that most of it comes via the pulpit, then we are missing out on something far more meaningful. If God within us is part and parcel of who we are, why are we giving more credence to other people's opinions than to the voice of God Himself within us? We ought to be super sensitive to His voice—obeying Him without hesitation. Although grace does not expect perfection from us, we should not mistake this freedom for permission to be disobedient. Prompt obedience to His voice is immensely profitable!

Without divine conversation, we become like wolf cubs. The mother wolf regurgitates semi-digested putrefied meat from her stomach to feed her cubs. Many believers are quite content with second hand putrefied regurgitated revelation. Sometimes the preacher has already fed from the regurgitation of other preachers. Now he re-regurgitates it once more for his congregation to feast on. Don't get me wrong, we do need mature guidance, but it is never the same as hearing first-hand from God. When we personally experience first-hand wisdom and guidance, it is so much more impactful—at times even Kairos moments upon which our destinies pivot.

In many circles, the clergy is regarded as a superior class of believer, but this is certainly not God's idea[18]. Jesus said that anyone wanting to be first must be servant of all[19].

By elevating the clergy to a super class outranking congregants, their blood bought privilege of being part and parcel of the "priesthood of believers" is surreptitiously usurped. This leaves ordinary believers with a third party connection to God—their divine intimacy, reduced to an arm's length arrangement with a distant God. When the clergy assumes the role of God's mediators, ordinary believers are defrauded of a divine romance. The thought of an arranged third-party mediation must be awfully disappointing to a God who created us for the purpose of one-on-one companionship with Himself. It is not only believers that are defrauded; God Himself is defrauded! In as much as we delight in first-hand intimacy, so does He! His kids are His pride and joy! Oh the delights of a divine romance! Can anything be more satisfying than the warmth of His embrace?

Think of it this way: In your intimate relationships with your new bride, would you prefer your best man to make love to her on your behalf? Well of course not! Such a notion is preposterous— the mere thought of it, distasteful! But it is just as repugnant for Jesus to have a third party clergy go-between relationship with His bride. You are His bride and He wants you all to Himself. To put it into an even more preposterous light, imagine that it's not your best man that stands in for you, but a paid professional. As preposterous as this sounds, there are many who expect paid religious leaders to perform such a service on their behalf. One can only imagine how repulsive it must be to our divine Lover.

It is interesting to note that He has promised never to leave us, but when we allow someone else to mediate with Him on our behalf, we are effectively distancing ourselves from Him. In doing so, we forfeit the joy of fellowshipping with our truest Friend.

We must accept that "We see through a glass darkly"[20]. Seeing that our understanding is always incomplete, shouldn't we always remain open, eager and ready to adjust our conclusions as He unveils more and more of His love and grace to us?

Whole denominations exist purely because they camped at their last revelation and did not move on with the cloud. Sadly, those involved in the last glorious move of God, very often oppose the next revelation and move of God.

Religion tells us that without the covering of a particular ministry, our revelation will fall into error. But if we choose to be covered by anyone other than Jesus, we are effectively replacing Him—choosing another man's revelation in favour of God's. In our day and age, with so many talented expositors of God's word, it is easy to be bamboozled by clever pulpiteering—leaving it up to them to hear God for us. But it is out of balance when we are told what God is saying more often than we are hearing God for ourselves.

Though we are accountable to Jesus alone; it does not follow that we are untouchable—no man is an island. We should all welcome guidance from our mentors and peers. There is a wealth of knowledge and experience to be shared with each other. But a problem arises when mentors are regarded as spiritual gurus and go-betweens.

When we are attentive to God's voice, and become accountable to Him alone, we have no need for go-betweens. Fatherly "covering" starts out innocently enough, but history has shown that it often regresses into slavish manipulation and control. It does not follow that covering will keep us out of error. It should be obvious that with covering we get someone else's errors. Thankfully, God is big enough to accommodate and overlook our many misunderstandings. That's what grace does. And thankfully, there is ample grace to cover my many misunderstandings—only God knows how desperately I am in need of His grace!

CONTROL GONE BERSERK

One of my previous pastors took a particularly hard line on an ex-worship leader who had chosen to live in homosexuality. Although he had already resigned from the church, the pastor still took measures to publicly ostracise him. One Sunday morning, he asked the congregation to stand up and make a public declaration, putting him out of fellowship, handing his body over to Satan so that his soul could be saved. Although he could find scripture for this, it seems the pastor did not take Matthew 18:17 into account. It says that we are to treat such a brother as a heathen. How should the church be treating heathen? By ostracizing them? Surely not! Aren't heathen the primary focus of the church? If we want to be more like Jesus, then surely, we should be welcoming heathen with open arms!

The worse the sinner, the more help is needed from the church. And, even though sinners may not be aware of it, let's face it, the church holds all the answers regarding every challenge anybody might be facing. How so? The church is supposed to be the dispenser of grace! It is not judgement but grace that is the ultimate solution to every ill of society! Grace is not dispensed for the purpose of allowing sin; it is dispensed for the purpose of fixing sinners! Although the church has the lifeline, it often drowns the very people they are trying to save. Criticism speaks louder than love. Sure, we all need to know what the Bible has to say about lifestyle choices, but other than by grace, there is no way to restore our fallen brothers. Let's face it, change doesn't come easy. Fortunately, grace, the most powerful force for change known to mankind, is strong enough to change us at heart level. Not only is condemnation awfully ungracious; it is also awfully un-gospel. There are spiritual repercussions, not only for those who are judged, but also for those who judge. Not only did this man die in a motor accident shortly after this incident, but the pastor responsible for this awful misjudgement also lost the mega-church he established.

Instead of cleansing the worship team, this Pharisaic attitude aroused sin within the team in the years that followed. The next worship team leader walked out of her marriage to run away with the team's guitarist. She was married to one of our associate pastors. He was immediately forced to step down from office—another ungracious blunder! She married the guitarist, then divorced him to have an affair with her sister's husband. They married and subsequently divorced. Sadly she died of cancer a short while later. Two worship team members and a youth pastor chose to live alternate sexual lifestyles. An associate pastor and worship team member left the church, then divorced and died shortly thereafter. One of the musicians may have been involved in serious fraud. Another associate pastor had an affair. Our subsequent senior pastor had an adulterous affair with one of our lady pastors, thereby destroying both their careers.

This church did not get this way because it was lax on moral teaching and congregational control. To the contrary, it got this way because it was overbearing, with little mercy for moral indiscretions! Contrary to what one may think; moral control is a devilish strategy! But this pastor didn't see it that way. He hardened his stance—preaching even more emphatically on chastity, virtue, moral standards, repentance and holiness. Sadly, as these virtuous demands abounded, they abounded at the expense of grace. And without grace, the church was powerless to bring about the morality it so earnestly sought. The senior pastor was vehemently opposed to what he labelled "extreme grace"—to him, it was no more than a licence to sin.

Where did they go wrong then? Holiness at the expense of grace is where they went wrong! Unfortunately, when grace is diluted with rules, grace is too watered down to play a meaningful role in bringing about godliness at heart level. Besides, when grace is made out to be conditional, it is no longer grace! If we dare to confront sin without grace, we confront sin without God, and without Him, there can be no holiness!

As strange as it may seem, the demand for virtue and morality did not improve morality, it stimulated immorality. 'But sin took advantage of this law and aroused all kinds of forbidden desires within me! If there were no law, sin would not have that power.' [21] The more prominence we give to Old Covenant commandments, the more we're enticed into sin.

When members must submit to laws and controls, the church is in danger of drowning in a backwash of ungodliness. In this church, control and the over emphasis of moral demands, led to the moral collapse of its leadership.

I regularly attended an early morning weekly men's prayer meeting in one of our member's homes. Sadly, it was shut down by church leadership because it had not been sanctioned by them. Aglow with the Spirit, these meetings were both refreshing and empowering. Members were sharing these blessings with surrounding churches—churches that were not accustomed to the supernatural manifestation of God's power. But the prayer meeting was not permitted to continue because it was not the senior pastor's idea.

In other instances, members have been instructed not to visit other churches. How limiting! I cannot help but ask the question, "Do we belong to the universal church of Christ, or to the empires of men?"

By contrast, I was in a meeting where the pastor told his congregation that he didn't want to see them in church Sunday after Sunday. He said that they should bless the surrounding churches of the city with their attendance and gifts. His theory was that if he and his congregation could build the kingdom of God in the city, he would not have to bother with building his own church—God would do that for him. The result was that his church became by far the biggest and most influential church in the city.

I once expressed my thoughts on grace in a letter to my pastor. The following weekend while barbequing at home with family and friends, my brother, an associate pastor at our church, told me a shocking story. At their last pastors' and elders' meeting, our senior pastor had stormed into the boardroom with my letter in his fist, angrily protesting that his authority had been challenged.

I was so taken aback with this shocking story that I immediately handed the barbeque tongs to my brother and sped off to the pastor's home.

He met me at the door, but did not invite me in. The tension was palpable. His cold reception left me bewildered. How could he possibly be offended by a letter meant to edify and support him in his noble ministry? But his deep seated religious paradigms would not allow him to see it for what it was—an encouragement from a devoted supporter of him and his fine ministry! Obviously, the concept of "religious fathering" affords status and privilege to the clergy. Grace simply cannot be accommodated within established religious hierarchy—it presents a challenge to the self-endowed religious status of the clergy, a threat to the status quo! I made no effort to convince him of my noble intent, choosing rather to take the high road—I apologised unconditionally and allowed him to have the last say.

Obviously I had touched a raw religious nerve. Perhaps he felt it presumptuous for a Financial Planner to comment on a matter of theology. Although the fierce reaction of someone I dearly love and respect had severely shaken me, I chose to grant him the grace I had written about and promised myself to not take offence. I was determined to wholeheartedly support him without reservation. I must be honest though, the innocence of our longstanding close relationship had been damaged, and I never regained the freedom to be honest with him again. Our fellowship became rather strained—I found myself measuring my every word—walking on egg shells—treading delicately in his presence. To put it plainly, although I didn't know it then, I had succumbed to religious witchcraft!

Instead of becoming more gracious, this pastor hardened his resolve to control his congregation all the more. One of his associate pastors told me that he had found the senior pastor at his home instructing his teenage daughter not to date a particular youth from the church on moral grounds. It turns out, the senior pastor's son was interested in having a relationship with her. This was an obvious case of misusing his authority—overstepping the bounds of decency. When the associate dared to object to his interference, he had no way of knowing what his objection would lead to. An oppressive atmosphere followed. Ultimately the relationship ran aground, culminating in the associate's resignation.

When the senior pastor took on the responsibility of ruling other people's lives, he just had too many balls in the air at the same time. Even jugglers can only manage a given number of balls at a time. He just kept on adding more balls until he had pushed his luck too far. That's when all the balls came raining down on his head.

His controlling ways became increasingly overbearing, to the point where more than half of his associate pastors resigned, leading to the biggest church split in the city's history.

This is an example of what happens when the pastor makes other people's private lives his responsibility. Anything less than the highest degree of meticulous crisis management, results in the entire house of cards crashing down into a shambolic heap. His grand scale of interference, in the name of "fathering", did not only alienate leaders and wreck relationships, but eventually put him out on the street without a soul to control. Ultimately, his controlling style of pastoring cost him the mega-church he had built from scratch.

The pastor who replaced him was one of the main movers and shakers in the South African Christian community. As a communicator of note, he very quickly wone the hearts and minds of the congregation.

But with the passage of time, his controlling spirit began to show through his charming personality. He would invite people to the front for prayer, and then with the microphone in their faces, instruct them to publically confess their sins. Besides being awfully embarrassing, these shocking exposés were damaging to families and relationships, leading to all kinds of humiliating complications. On some occasions, the sheer pressure of having a microphone thrust before them, would cause them to blurt out ill-chosen words with far reaching consequences. Like a deer caught in the headlights, a dignified lady confessed to fornication when she meant to say covetousness. How could she even begin to undo the damage after the scandal mongers added their bit?

His strategy did nothing to purify the congregation. The only thing that his fear motivation achieved was to make his congregation more conscious of their sin than of their righteous standing with God. Paul put it this way: The law gives sin its power[21]. Ultimately, the Pastor's controlling ways backfired on him. His sincere attempt at eradicating sin from the congregation, served only to stimulate sin in the camp.

He made an appeal to unmarried youth to come forward and verbally commit their lives to sexual purity. He had them repeat after him a vow not to touch members of the opposite sex. He then informed them that if they were to break their promise, dire divine consequences would follow. To seal their commitments, he quoted an Old Testament curse reserved for covenant breakers. Sounds right doesn't it?

The problem is that they were not able to keep their promises, and consequently fell into remorse and shame. Shame prevents people from communing with God. Instead of cleansing the youth, he succeeded only in igniting an irresistible passion for each other. In the process, healthy relationships turned into sinful relationships, resulting in a sense of personal guilt, unworthiness and shame. This is all it took to spoil what had once been vibrant personal relationships with their heavenly Father.

He would make controlling statements from the pulpit like, "If I ever catch anybody in the congregation making passes at another man's wife, I will personally 'donner' him" (beat him up violently—Afrikaans). Although he was making his point rather light heartedly, he was preaching the problem rather than the solution, and in the process, inadvertently distorting the fine character of God in the minds of his congregation.

One day he told his congregation that he had told God that if ever he were to commit adultery, that God should strike him dead with lightening. Later, I had opportunity to take this matter up with him. I felt that in suggesting that God would strike people dead with lightening for sinning, he was inadvertently giving his congregation the wrong impression of God's fine character.

He explained to me that what He had said to God was a private matter between him and God, and had nothing to do with me. But he could not deny that, since sharing it with the congregation, he had made it every member's business—as a result, they had all come to believe that their God was ungracious.

It wasn't too long after this incident that the elders made a public announcement. This highly esteemed senior pastor and one of his associate lady pastors had resigned from their posts and left town. The two of them had been in an adulterous relationship. The congregation was blissfully unaware of the affair. To them, he and his wife seemed happily married.

Those who demand legalism from others are obviously living by legalism themselves. Legalism puts the onus on the individual to live up to a prescribed code. But nobody is capable of keeping up the pace. Satan uses legalism to entrap those practicing it. He waits for an opportunity. Then, when their guard is down, he ensnares them in the very things they so desperately try to resist. But God does not expect us to change ourselves—that's the work of the Holy Spirit. Without grace, there can be no fruit of the Spirit—His fruit is dispensed with grace!

SELECTIVE SELFISHNESS

Brian, an author on the subject of grace and his wife, Jane, moved to a large city and joined a lively congregation. They felt accepted and at home and just knew that this was the place that God had chosen for them. The honeymoon with the new congregation continued for two glorious years.

Unfortunately all of that changed after they introduced an elderly couple to the church. They too felt very much at home there and made a commitment to become members at the next new member intake.

At that time, their family was in crisis—their grandson was on life support and not expected to live very much longer. You can imagine their desperation, but fortunately, they had found a caring community where they could ask for prayer and get moral and spiritual support.

They approached one of the pastors for prayer. The answer they got from him left them speechless. The Pastor refused to pray for the child, saying that they should ask for prayer at the church where the child's parents attended. Stunned by his rebuff, this gentle old couple were at a loss for words. Reeling under the shock of such unexpected rejection, at a loss for words, they failed to mention that the child's parents did not go to any church at all.

Some months previously the senior pastor had stated very firmly from his pulpit that the church would commit itself to those who were committed to the church, and that those who were not committed should not expect the church to commit to them. To Brian and Jane's surprise, the congregation enthusiastically chorused their approval. They trusted their pastor sufficiently to take him at his word, and didn't perceive un-Christlikeness in his stance. This was religion at its best, convincing a whole congregation into believing that un-grace was God's way of doing things.

A visiting pastor had made a very opposite statement from the same pulpit. He had said that the church was the only institution on earth that existed for the benefit of its non-members. How refreshing to hear this from the same pulpit. Unfortunately his enlightened view went down like a lead balloon with the senior pastor. Religion will not allow something to be given for no good reason at all—that's too much like grace, and in order for grace to be grace, it would have to be given to those who do not deserve it!

The leader of the church's businessmen's fellowship invited Brian to be the speaker at the forthcoming Thursday morning get-together. Just before the meeting, plans changed, and another speaker was arranged. Brian did not suspect anything untoward. He was informed that he would be slotted in at a later date. After not hearing from them for some months, he enquired as to when they would require him to speak. He was given a date. Still not suspecting anything contrary, he agreed.

The night before he was to speak, he awoke shortly after midnight with a start. The Lord revealed to him that the church had decided not allow him to speak that morning. He woke Jane and told her what the Lord had shown him. After that, sleep was impossible.

Forewarned, Brian wondered how the church would break the news to him at the meeting. They said nothing. Although the style of these businessman's meetings was not "praise and worship centred", the leader kept urging the guitarist to continue with worship. He stretched it out to the end of the service, leaving no time for the message. It was obvious that they did not want their people to hear what Brian had to say about God's goodness and grace, but were not brave enough to tell him. He was never invited to speak again.

Later, Brian had reason to phone the pastor to comment on a point he had made in a sermon. He barely started making his point when the pastor interrupted him, accusing him of heresy, saying that he was a heretic and that his books were heresy, and that's why he wouldn't read them. Brian couldn't help wondering how he could have come to such a conclusion without reading them. The pastor suggested that, upon Brian's return from his holiday in New Zealand, he find another church, recommending the Presbyterians.

Brian and Jane were left in a state of utter shock and disbelief. The pastor had always been so caring and welcoming, but now his true feelings towards them were gushing out in torrents of animosity. He went on to say that every time he saw Brian, he wanted to run a mile! Brian and Jane had no idea that he had felt this way—they didn't see it coming—they were often warmly received by the pastor. Now it was apparent that his kindness had been insincere. Shockingly, the care and love they had so appreciated from his hands had been nothing more than a sham!

Brian and Jane had cheerfully invested so much of themselves into the lives of congregants—they love this pastor and these people dearly. What was this all about? Shaken, confused and bewildered— at a loss to know who to turn to for help!

Brian made the fatal mistake of confiding in a trusted friend who also happened to be a member of the church. Unbeknown to Brian, he went straight to the pastor. Next, Brian received a very angry phone call from the pastor, saying that if Brian continued to speak to any of his congregants, he would make a public announcement at the next service to denounce him as a heretic. He would forbid his members from reading his books, and not allow them to have anything to do with him, either personally or in business. This blistering barrage came from the man who had won their hearts. They could not believe that their loving pastor could resort to blackmail. One cannot begin to imagine their shock!

Is this pastor a bad man? Not at all! He is a good man called of God, yet caught up in a bad religious system. He may be thinking, "How can my practices be wrong if they were passed down to me by the highly respected fathers of my denomination?" He is sincerely convinced that God appointed him to keep his congregants pure. Sadly, he chose to achieve his mission by the ungraciousness of anger, manipulation and control.

Are you offended by the duplicity of this story? Has it made you suspicious of your pastor? This is not a time for suspicion; this is a time for love and support. No pastor on the face of the earth has a perfect grip on pastoring. Pastors can do with all the support we can give them. We have a role to play, and that role is not to stand in judgement; it is to show support and grace, whether deserved or not.

Brian and Jane left on holiday for New Zealand in a state of extreme emotional numbness. On their travels, in the weeks that followed, there was little chance for a good night's sleep—every quiet moment was filled with the unbearable pain of rejection.

Then, while touring New Zealand, the unexpected happened. Early one morning, Jane awoke with a look of stark terror in her eyes. She asked Brian where they were. Brian answered, "Whitianga". Her next question was, "Where are we?" Brian thought this rather odd, but patiently answered, "Whitianga". Her next question was, "Where are we?" And this went on repeatedly—the same question followed by the same answer. After an uncountable number of repeats, she eventually asked how they had gotten there. Now extremely concerned, Brian answered, "In Stewie's car." The next question was, "How did we get here?" Again, the same question followed by the same answer was repeated many times.

By this time, Brian was beside himself with distress!

"Had my wonderful wife turned into a mindless imbecile?"

He thought he would test her by saying, "We're here to visit our grandchild." The surprise in her eyes was obvious, "I have a grandchild?" she asked in disbelief. By now terror had gripped Brian by the throat. He felt as though a steel band was squeezing the air out of his lungs. He began to probe with simpler questions, which to his dismay, she was unable to answer. Then in a panic, she began to cry hysterically. She was utterly lost, not knowing who she was, where they were, or that she had children and grandchildren. She was a person without a past and she could not grasp the simple information Brian was giving her. Her mind was grappling for anything that could help her understand what was happening—anything that could give her back her identity.

Stunned and bewildered, Brian went through to the bathroom and called on the Lord, "What has happened to my wonderful wife? Would she ever regain her sanity?" It seemed their relationship could never be normal again. Deeply troubled, he wondered what a life with an imbecile would be like—would our grandchildren ever have the privilege of knowing how wonderful their loving granny was?

Later that day, snippets of memory began to return to her. Whitianga is on the rugged Coromandel Peninsula, far from any kind of medical facility. It was half a day's drive to the nearest facility on the opposite side of the mountainous peninsula. The day was almost over when they reached the small town of Thames and its tiny hospital. The Arab doctor called for every possible blood and neurological test imaginable, and came up with the diagnosis of "confusion brought on by anxiety".

After this, they made their way to friends in Auckland. Their friend, a non-practicing professional nurse, was not at all impressed with the diagnosis, and insisted that they not leave Auckland until they had gotten to the bottom of Jane's confusion.

The next day they took her to a doctor who redid all the tests, but could not come up with a diagnosis. Instead, he referred her to a neurologist at another hospital.

Once again, the neurologist did his tests and left them wondering what this was all about. Later he returned with a diagnosis. Jane had survived a very rare condition called "Transient Global Amnesia". It was so rare that he had only encountered it twice in his long medical career. It is a condition of temporary memory loss during which a person is not able to form new memories. This explained why she had asked the same questions repeatedly. After asking a question, she was immediately unable to remember that she had asked the question. Her words instantly vaporised from her memory, never to be remembered again.

There is one good thing about Transient Global Amnesia. When the episode passes, it is impossible to remember that the episode actually occurred. Jane was simply left with a gap in her memory that will never be regained.

Transient Global Amnesia isn't easily triggered—it takes an unusually severe life altering shock to set it off. The delayed shock of having such wonderful close church friends turn against them, was just too much for Jane to handle. They returned to South Africa with a wad of New Zealand medical bills.

They thought that the church had had its say, and that friendships with their close church friends would continue as before, but they were in for yet another shock. Church friends took their calls courteously enough, promising to phone back, but alas, never did. Business deals that Brian had concluded with church members were mysteriously cancelled.

Brian and Jane's disillusionment with religion had finally been sealed. Although they have forgiven all the parties concerned and continue to pray for God to richly bless them, it took them two long years to finally shake the affair out of their systems and return to a state of something resembling normality.

Religion doesn't know, or worse still, doesn't care what damage it wreaks on those it rejects. Religion has a way of making one feel welcome, loved and at home, but a flimsy friendship precariously balanced on a knife's edge, is not really friendship at all! When love fails, we must ask ourselves if it was actually love in the first place. After all, didn't Paul say that love never fails[37]?

Their parting could just as easily have been amicable. After all, brothers are family, aren't they? Surely it could at least have ended with mutual respect. But the hostility of their dear friend and loving pastor was palpable!

If it is true to say that grace is the ultimate expression of real love, then it is obvious that excommunication is clear evidence of un-grace—not something our loving Lord Jesus would do! How awfully painful it was for Brian and Jane to come to terms with outright rejection—especially when it came from the very man they so dearly admired. Obviously, the "fatherly love" they had experienced from his hands had been far from real. If love can flip over into animosity at the drop of a hat, can it really be love at all? Yes, many accept the actions of their beloved pastors as actions of love. They would not expect less from trusted fathers of the faith. How is it possible that leaders' actions can be so blatantly at odds with the love of our Lord Jesus?

Disagreements are inevitable—churches are comprised of people, and wherever there are people, there will be misunderstandings. But what was of particular concern was that the church ceased to care whether their brother and sister survived or drowned in the backwash of their animosity. How does the love of God fit into such anger?

Obviously, the love and grace that Brian wrote about had been perceived to be at odds with the Pastor's theology, and he took exception to it, seeing it as a challenge to his authority.

This precious congregation had been hoodwinked into accepting that love could be dispensed with ungraciousness. Sadly, they had not grasped the concept of the love that Paul described in his first letter to the Corinthians[37]. But praise God! Regardless of their hostility, there is still ample grace for all concerned. I trust that, rather than take offence, you understand that ungraciousness cannot be fixed with ungraciousness!

Satan works undercover—he is so cunning that he is seldom found out. The commendable religious practice of spiritual fathering is often hijacked by him. He takes the gap, using seemingly benign religious father figures to gain control of innocent church members. The seemingly benign practice of fathering provides a perfect camouflage for manipulation and control. In the Galatian church, Paul identified this dark practice as bewitchment[5]. Precious souls seldom notice that they have fallen prey to it, especially when scripture is used to legitimise ungraciousness. This kind of fathering is often carried out with legalism. Sadly, as legalism increases, more and more power devolves upon the clergy. And when this happens, beware! Manipulation has arrived! Seldom obvious—rather sneaky and surreptitious. Additionally, clerical actions must not be questioned— the dignity of their office must at all times be defended. There are clergy who demand blind submission to them and their ideas. They present themselves as "God's appointed father figures"—a wonderful sounding religious idea, but a diabolical ploy that disinherits innocent followers—a ploy that has little regard for the liberty for which Jesus died. Innocent followers are simply defrauded of their freedom in the interests of "holiness!"

Legalism convinces its followers that God's attention can be gained through rule keeping. It cannot allow believers the luxury of relying exclusively upon the free gift of righteousness bestowed upon them at rebirth.

No matter how sincere our striving for God's love and favour through rule keeping may be, it presents no threat to Satan's devilish schemes—he is a past master at playing religious games. If he can keep us running on religion, he can keep us from discovering that we are already entirely loved just as we are. He also knows that the futility of self-change will lead to hypocrisy. To make up for unresolved weaknesses, congregants settle for conjuring up saintly images. We'll do whatever it takes to find acceptance in our particular group. A pious front will do—at least it allows us to fit in!

The more we are pressured into striving for personal change, the more guilt and unworthiness we reap. Guilt and unworthiness lead to wobbly faith. "Oh, what the heck! Everybody else is doing it." So we settle for a form of godliness and resign ourselves to grin and bear a powerless gospel[38]. "But so what! Nobody needs to know about our unconquered sins—they can remain hidden". Duplicity fits in perfectly with Satan's deceitful plans.

With so much shallowness going around, those who can pretend best become the judges of those who have difficult pretending. But pious pretence is nothing more than pantomime, and pantomime is certainly not holiness!

If sincere believers can be persuaded to give father figures the right to hear God for them, they soon come to lean more heavily upon priestly father figures, than upon their heavenly Father. Rather than being Spirit led, they give father figures the right to call the shots—what to believe, what to do, and when to do it. Then when it comes to life's major decisions, they don't have the confidence to decide for themselves. In the process, their individuality is sacrificed in the cause of "shepherding". Instead of rising up as authority taking devil busters, they jump to the whims of manipulators. But God is not looking for clones. Our individuality and quirks make us unique. There is nothing lovable about regimented conformity; it's our idiosyncrasies and oddities that endear us to one another. And God is no less taken with our uniqueness, accepting each of His beloved children just as they are. He loves variety—we see it in the extravagance of His creation.

What is it that distinguishes a church from a cult? It is the degree to which personal control has devolved into the hands of a strong leader. Satan regards mind control as first prize—it is how he gets good honest believers to fall under his spell. The "Jones Town" cult would not have convinced nine hundred and twelve innocent followers to commit suicide, unless it had first taken them down the slippery pathway of mind control. Believers beware! You may not be persuaded to commit suicide for your leader, but you may find yourself at the mercy of his whims.

The Jones Town tragedy is not unique. Church leaders may feel the need to control their flocks in the commendable interests of "holiness". Although done with the very best of intensions; manipulation is certainly not God's way—it plays directly into the enemy's hands.

Unbeknown to Brian and Jane, the freedom they had found in God's grace had been perceived to be a challenge to the church's established control of its people. Legalism and grace are diametrically opposite—they cannot be blended. A judgemental paradigm is simply not capable of understanding a mercy and grace paradigm. The concept of freedom is just too foreign a concept to be grasped by those who feel divinely compelled to control. By its very nature, legalism will always view grace with suspicion.

Brian and Jane's rejection could not be chalked up to a clash of personalities. It was the aftermath of a battle fought in the heavenlies. Not every confrontation in the heavenlies has a happy ending. Fortunately, Brian and Jane believe that their tragic story is for a greater purpose. They continue to expect something good to come out of it.

What is your reaction to this unfortunate tale? Is it anger and revenge, or mercy and grace? Does it make you want to destroy bridges or to build bridges? Never forget who the enemy is—it's not church leaders—they can do with all the help, support and understanding we can give. This is not a time for offense taking; it is a time for understanding—a time to ratchet up our level of graciousness to them. Love covers a multitude of sins.

I have included this story, not to discredit God's anointed leaders, but to discredit the fallacious practice of legalism—it is out to steal our liberty freedom and grace. Authoritarianism is a devilish ploy to destroy the work of Jesus from within. From the perspective of God's grace, it seems so obviously un-Christlike, yet many embrace it as though it is godliness. Before we know it, we have slipped into the clutches of religiousness—after all, how can it be wrong if it was passed down to us by respected men and women of God?

If you are going to confront ungraciousness, take special care: Ungraciousness cannot be confronted with ungraciousness. If we received the treasure of grace by personal revelation, then we need to have the grace to allow personal revelation to do its work in our leaders. Our responsibility is to love and support them, and to trust God to do the rest.

Often believers who have discovered freedom in grace, have simply been brow beaten back into submission to legalism. Others, who have tried swimming against the current, have ultimately given in to the relentless pressure, and gone with the flow of legalism. It is so much easier to tow the religious line—with it comes the approval of our brothers and sisters. In sheer disillusionment, others have dropped out of the conventional way of doing church, never to cast their shadow across the threshold of a church door again.

According to a survey, more Christians do not attend church than those who do. Non-church attending believers make up 58% of all Christians. I was sceptical of these statistics, so I conducted my own mini survey to see if there was any substance to them. My Grandfather started a church in the 1920s. All of his six children and their children attended his church regularly. Most of the 133 of his offspring to the sixth generation are believers. In my mini survey of family members, I came to almost the same statistic. 57% of believers in my grandfather's family do not attend church.

I firmly believe that a lack of grace is largely responsible for this sad state of affairs. Religion may reach out with grace to the unsaved masses, but thereafter give grace a distorted twist—you have to put your life right—the beady eye of religious oversight is watching you!

The only reward for our ineffective religious efforts is guilt. It is guaranteed—our sincerest attempts at holiness will fail, and with failure comes shame. Sadly, shame leads to anything from acceding to the pressure and toeing the religious company line, to bucking the system in rebellion! Some may succumb, and others may fall away into a "couldn't care less" attitude. Does religion really care about the casualties it leaves in its wake? If you have been trashed by religion, you know the answer to that question.

Unity is one of the core tenants of Christianity. Religion, on the other hand, does not unite—to the contrary, religion segments and divides—the reason for so many denominations. Satan's chief strategy is to divide and conquer—we see it clearly demonstrated in denominationalism. Religion often provides acceptance, love and care, provided we are prepared to put down our personal identity and assume the identity of the group. Fresh insights are welcomed, provided they fit neatly into prevailing denominational paradigms. But beware if they don't—the ungracious practice of Christian shunning is bound to follow!

When religion takes on the role of accuser, "the accuser of the brethren's" work is done! Let's be honest—love without grace is not the love Jesus lived and taught. His love was drenched in grace! Anything less, is no more than the shallow practice of "selective selfishness".

Love is something that is given unconditionally, while "selective selfishness" is something that is done in the guise of love, but with a devilish twist—it has reciprocation in mind! In other words, it comes with strings attached. According to Jesus, we should not expect a pat on the back for merely reciprocating good for good—even unbelievers do that[74].

The God kind of agape love says, "I expect nothing in return for the care I give you", while selective selfishness says, "I offer you care and affection provided there is something in it for me." Let's not kid ourselves—to be loved in this shallow way is not really being loved at all. If love is given to obtain something in return, it is not grace; it is extortion!

On the surface, these two forms of relationships appear to be identical—most people never discover religion's duplicitous use of the word "love". Sadly, once people have settled for superficiality, they find it difficult to accept that God's love can be any different.

In order to know which form of caring is practiced by a particular group, one should not ask those within the group; one should ask those who have become casualties of the group. The question to ask them is, "Are the ties of love that once embraced you, still embracing you?" After all, according to Paul, "love never ceases"[37].

I have included Brian and Jane's story, not to raise your hackles, but to make the distinction between religion and grace a little clearer. My hope is that you will embrace grace and be more aware of the snares that accompany the "pious" practise of un-grace.

I appeal to you most sincerely—please do not adopt any offence from this story. Grace cannot be fostered in ungracious ways. My hope is that this sad tale of ungraciousness will give you all the more reason to be gracious at every opportunity. Take special care to be gracious in your campaign for grace!

ANSWER TO A DUMB PRAYER

We relocated to a small coastal town and joined a lively church. It didn't take us too long to settle in and become fully involved with church activities. At the time I began to write books on the subject of grace, and passed my first manuscript out to a few pastor friends for comments and suggestions. I also sent a copy to our new pastor. I received encouragement from all except our pastor. I imagined that he was simply too busy to find time for it.

Then, some months later, he phoned and asked me to visit him in his office. I left home with a buoyant sense of anticipation—eager to get his encouragement. On arrival, I was greeted rather frostily and ushered into his office. I stepped into a frigid atmosphere, and was strategically seated before three pastors. The last thing I had expected was a hostile reception. I was at a loss to imagine what had led to this.

The senior pastor opened the discussion with an accusation, "Deon you have slandered me", and went on to repeat his accusation again and again. He was enormously offended by my views on grace. It seemed obvious that he had misconstrued my enthusiasm for grace to be an attack on his ministry. At that time I had no idea that grace could be offensive to anybody. It perplexed me—how could he possibly have confused my desire to spread God's love to be an attack on His ministry? The barrage of accusations on me continued for two heart breaking hours. I could not convince the pastors that my manuscript was intended to make believers more conscious of God's love for them. I was naive enough to think that they would welcome my endeavour.

Devastated and bewildered; I left his office with my tail between my legs, not knowing what to do next.

I went directly to the Lord to enquire from Him. His answer was immediate and clear. I was to continue to serve the congregation with the same loving grace that I had written about. Despite the pastor's antagonism, I decided to make a wholehearted commitment to support him and his fine work.

Over a period of some months, more meetings with the pastor followed, each equally accusatory of my view on grace. But through it all, with God's help, I was able to remain calm, responding to their anger with as much grace I could muster. After each meeting, shattered and disillusioned, I would call on the Lord, and each time got the same answer. "Respond to their anger with grace—the same grace you wrote about." Finally, after the last meeting with them, the Lord showed me clearly that our season with that congregation had finally come to an end. We made sure, at least from our side, that we left on the very best of terms.

At the end of the day I had no one to blame but myself for initiating this unhappy sequence of events. It all started with my dumb prayer. I had prayed, "Lord let them discover your grace, even if it costs us rejection." What was I thinking? Had I known just how costly these words would turn out to be, I would have chosen my words a little more carefully. If it had only affected me, it would have been one thing, but that it affected my family was more than I had bargained for. Dumb prayers sure can be costly!

At that point, I had only received half the answer to my prayer. I had asked for rejection and got it in truck loads. We patiently continued to wait for the balance of my prayer to be answered— namely that these lovely folk would come to discover how gracious their heavenly Father really is.

We had to wait about three or four years before the answers began to roll in. We attended a week long grace conference in Cape Town with Rob Rufus, pastor of City Church International, Hong Kong. We desperately needed to hear from God, and Rob's wonderful understanding of God's love and grace confirmed that our mission to spread the word of His goodness was still on track. Nothing could be more edifying than feasting on God's love.

During a tea break, someone behind me tapped me on the shoulder. As I turned to see who it was, I found myself in the bear hug of a very strong man. It was the son-in-law of the Pastor who had taken offence at my manuscript. At the time, he and his wife were also offended by my understanding of God's goodness, and would never have set foot in a grace conference, but here they were at a full blown grace conference, and he was hugging a full on grace junky. He let me go and then hugged me twice more.

"Hello Paul—what's up my friend?" I asked in surprise. I was not only surprised to be hugged by someone who had rejected us and our message, but also surprised that he would be interested in travelling a thousand kilometres to hear a grace teacher speaking on the very subject that he had reckoned to be heresy.

"Deon, you will never guess what has happened to us. We have become grace people." You could have knocked me over with a feather.

"I don't understand Paul—you and your family were so vehemently against it."

"Yes, but you got us thinking. Eventually the penny dropped and we saw it clearly for ourselves. Now we are completely sold out to grace."

"What are you telling me Paul? This has got to be the best news I have heard in a long time."

"The news gets even better Deon. My father-in-law has done an about turn and embraces grace in a big way. You won't recognise his ministry—it's pure grace."

"And his congregation—are they okay with grace?"

"Oh Deon, that's the sad part. After so many years of legalism, the church was unable take a leap of faith with him. The gap between the gospel of performance and the gospel of grace was just too big for them to breach. He no longer pastors there, but don't worry about him, he is a changed man. When his eyes were eventually opened to the liberation that grace brings, he made a doctrinal U-turn. His messages are so different now—saturated with love and grace."

"Wow! Is that right?" Now on cloud nine—barely able to contain the joy I was feeling! "Paul, I am delighted to hear the news!"

As if this encounter was not enough, we bumped into another pastor friend at the conference. He was from a different congregation in our old home town. Previously, when we had discussed grace, he had not understood what I was going on about, and had thought my ideas to be completely off the wall.

"Hi Richard! Isn't this a surprise! A grace conference is the last place I would have expected to find you—don't tell me that you have also bought into this weird grace message?"

"You better believe it Deon! Although we thought you were way off- beam, your odd ideas got us thinking, and we eventually discovered the way of grace for ourselves." I was blown away with gratitude for God's faithfulness.

"Excuse me for my surprise, but I have heard two similar stories in one day—I am stoked!"

I left there floating on cloud nine—my heart bursting with thankfulness—this was about as much good news as I could handle in one day.

So many answers to prayer all at once! At last, years of painful rejection had paid off. These dear folk had finally got the message of how unconditionally they are loved. God does answer prayer— even dumb prayers, and I have no doubt that more answers will follow!

These lovely folk can be excused for putting us through the wringer. The truth is that legalism leads to judgementalism, and judgementalism does not understand mercy—they are conflicting paradigms—the one is rigid and unbending, while the other is empathetic and understanding—the one must be deserved, while the other cannot be deserved. With grace comes freedom, something that religion cannot afford to allow in its ranks.

They say that if you love someone, you can never be entirely certain that they love you, unless they have the freedom to leave you. Only if they return can you be sure that you are truly loved. Grace gives us that freedom—a freedom to validate our love for our heavenly Father. Conversely, the kind of "love" that is given, simply because it is expected, will always lack sincerity. But if we choose to stay when we have the freedom to leave, it is obvious that our hearts have been captured. With grace we love, not because we must, but because we are in love! The sincerity of this kind of affection is all the more convincing to the One receiving it.

Religious bewitchment is not always obvious. Sometimes it is so subtle that it is mistaken for love. In the harsh reality of a loveless world, people are often desperate to find acceptance. When they find it in a church community, they are likely to open their hearts, thus making themselves susceptible to the religion of the day.

When it comes to counselling, rules are often liberally doled out. Sounds right, doesn't it? But as children of the Most High God, we have much more than sheer dogged determination and human resolve at our disposal; we are equipped with mighty weapons of spiritual warfare for the bringing down of strongholds. We are divinely empowered to be more than conquerors! People are looking to us for something bigger than themselves. They are not looking for rules, they are looking for godly direction and divine empowerment—all of which is contained in grace! If counselling is not grace based, it is works based, and that is plain and simply a form of humanism—a country mile short of the grace of Jesus!

Just as you can tell the age of a tree by counting the concentric rings on its cross section, so you can tell the age of a denomination by counting the number of religious traditions they observe. Most denominations start out with a fresh move of God. The great church reformations had their beginnings in grace. They led the church out of dead works and traditions into the effervescent life of the Spirit. Although initially established in grace, each subsequent generation diluted the vibrancy of grace a little more with dead religion, until grace lost all significance. Religion is toxic!

Satan is very sneaky—he has his own agenda—he does all he can to crowd grace out—offering empty religion in its place. Then when grace resurfaces, religion feels threatened, and does all it can to preserve the status quo. It is a historical fact—the grace that Paul taught, slowly but surely regressed to the point to where it became no more than empty religious routines, profoundly devoid of the power of grace. When intimacy with God becomes a ceremony about Him, rather than a loving romance with Him, we have reduced God in our lives, and have nothing of real value to offer the world.

When leaders adopt the role of spiritual mediators for the masses, ordinary believers cease to walk in their God given authority. Eventually the miraculous is no longer normal, and anything supernatural is treated with scepticism. In many cases, God ordained dominion and authority has slipped out of the hands of believers into the hands of leadership. Under these circumstances, intimate interaction with God dims over time, until eventually all passion is washed out of divine romance. Let's face it, genuflects and order of service do not impress God—He is interested in our companionship, not our etiquette!

As new creatures in Christ, God is inseparably part and parcel of who we are, accompanying us everywhere we go[67]. He is present with us when we are naked and in the most undignified moments of our ablutions. He is happy to communicate with us at these times, and does so without the slightest flinch of embarrassment.

He is no less with us when we are sinning, than when we are worshipping. He does not fall in and out of love with us in accordance with our behaviour.

As already stated. Adam and Eve's sin did not sever God's relationship with them—it was their shame that did it. After they had sinned, it was them that hid from God; not God that hid from them. From God's side, the relationship was still perfectly intact. He came looking for them, wanting to continue communing with them in the cool of the day as before, but they could not bear the thought of facing Him—their sense of unworthiness got in the way[108]. Although God's love for them continued to burn just as intensely; they were so blinded by their shame that they imagined that He no longer had any reason to love them. Well here's the bottom line—the fact that they could not grasp the graciousness of the relationship, did not make the relationship any less gracious.

Shame is destructive—it causes us to avoid God. We can so easily allow shame to rob us of intimacy—it puts distance into romance. Although certainly not the case, nonetheless shame puts distance between us and our most loyal ally and dearest Friend.

NO THANKS! I CAN MAKE MYSELF RIGHT

I Can Make Myself Right—fact or fiction? I have a friend whose son is a thief. Despite a lifetime of regular church attendance, a year at a Christian rehabilitation centre in a foreign land, and a night in jail, he is still a thief. His father asked him to house-sit his home while he and his mother were abroad. Upon their return, stuff was missing. But his son had a cock and bull story to explain the loss.

He would struggle to find a job, but no sooner employed, he would be stealing from his employer. His younger brothers did what they could to convince his employer not to press charges. After his father died, he continued to steal from his aging mother who was already in a pitiful financial state. He would thrill her heart by paying her a visit, and then break her heart when she would discover more things missing from her home.

Pawnshops would only give him a fraction of an item's true value, while his mother would have to pay dearly to replace her losses. Sometimes his brothers would rescue stolen items from pawnshops at their own expense. At other times, when they were not able to afford the redemption, the item would simply be forfeited.

Despite being a pastor's kid with a firm grounding in the word, a lifetime of church attendance, exorcism, multiple recommitments,

Christian counselling, discipleship, rehabilitation, family help and financial bailouts, he was simply not able to change himself.

Broken promises upon broken promises, yet his wife stayed faithful to him. Despite dragging her through all kinds of embarrassments, she slogged on, doing her best to provide a living from her meagre wage.

But eventually he pushed his luck too far. Lies upon lies had smothered out the last smouldering embers of any thought of reformation. He had used and abused friends and family, and taken their support and hand-outs for granted. The effort of covering for him was taking its toll on his wife's sanity. After tolerating so much, she was left with no alternative, but to step out of his life permanently.

Her mother took her under her wing, shielding her from any contact with him, knowing that if he were to communicate with her, he would lie his way back into her heart. One would think that this would be enough to bring him to his senses, but that would be expecting too much—his deviant ways continued.

He is fit, talented, personable, good looking, and strange as it may seem, a likeable fellow. He is a lover of life and dreams of better times to come. He had everything going for him, except trust, and without trust he had absolutely nothing at all. He turned over so many new leaves—he tried so hard, but no matter how sincere his resolve, his efforts were never enough. He couldn't shake the monkey off his back.

Some of us have learnt how to camouflage our less than wholesome thoughts and feelings with a socially acceptable level of behaviour, but in truth, we have no way of changing our hearts. Our hearts are the control centres from which both good and bad behaviour is dictated[94].

We refer to certain successful individuals as self-made men. Booksellers have whole gondolas loaded with books on the subject. I did a Google search on "Self-Help" and came up with nine hundred and five million websites. The world is saying, "We can do this ourselves—we don't need God". Self-Help is one of the world's great billion-dollar industries. With so much help around, why is poverty, suicide, unhappiness, broken relationships and crime on the increase? It doesn't add up—something seriously amiss!

Religion has been going at it for thousands of years longer than any modern-day self-help guru, and yet has an equally dismal record. Obviously religion just doesn't work, but religious folk just don't seem to get it! Believe me—I have been at it for long enough to know.

One would expect its followers to be people of honour. Anyone who has been in business for any length of time will know that, by and large, Christians are just as likely to let one down in business as non-Christians.

The divorce rate is higher among Christians than non-Christians. When a Christian convention comes to town, the sale of pornography goes up in that city. What does that say about religion? Its ideals may be commendable, but unless it presents grace as the solution to sin, it remains a work of the flesh—a country mile short of the glorious gospel of Jesus.

If the message Sunday after Sunday encourages us to live better lives, then why don't we live better? Yes, outwardly we appear to live better, but tread on our toes and you get a clearer idea of how effective our religion actually is. Courtesy, charm and politeness may be able to camouflage our anger momentarily, but that doesn't mean that underlying anger isn't lurking just below the surface, ready to pounce if pushed too far. Yes, there is a place for righteous anger. No, there is no place for selfish anger. All too often, we excuse our anger; claiming it to be righteously justified. Like people of the world, we think we have a right to use anger to get our way, even though such worldly thinking is foreign to the kingdom.

Interdenominational animosity and inter-clerical rivalry indicates at best, mistrust, and at worst, a struggle for denominational dominance. Either way, wearing a collar backwards does not change an offender into a paragon of virtue. We are all offenders at different points on the road of sanctification—nobody is perfect. The clergy is made up of humanity, and humanity comes with all its weaknesses. There is a danger of imagining that they are less vulnerable than we. When the clergy are backed into a corner, we soon get to know how effective their religion is. The purveyors of religion are in the same rickety boat as those who dutifully follow their teachings.

I happened to be in a banking hall when a clergyman lost his temper with a bank staffer. The quiet buzz of conversation from the long queues fell silent as his loud ranting got the whole hall's attention. His priestly identity may have remained secret if he hadn't foolishly blurted out, "Do… you… know… who… you… are… speaking… to? I… am… doctor... pastor…(………..)" (he shall remain nameless). As if his titles should count for some kind of superior treatment. Didn't Christ say that he who wants to be first should be a servant to all[19]?

It turns out that his wild ranting was over a matter so trivial that nothing more than a little courtesy would have been sufficient to straighten things out, but he chose to swat a fly with a sledge hammer. When using a sledge hammer, one should always ensure that the fly is not sitting on a windowpane. In this case the windowpane was the timid little lady bank clerk—a fragile windowpane so easily shattered—still in tears long after he had left. What a bully—he could have picked on someone his own size. There were other windowpanes shattered that day. The crowded banking hall could not believe what they had just witnessed. What a monster! What a pious blunderer! What a pompous pastor! What a fine job he did of winning the lost that day.

If he was looking for a congregation to preach to, this was his finest hour—he had the attention of the crowd. I am sure that they would have loved to have heard his sermon on "turning the other cheek", or maybe the one about "the good Samaritan". On second thoughts, I don't think either would have gone down too well that day.

In his eruption of arrogance, it was not the weeping bank clerk who was discredited, but the conceited Pharisee. His pomposity preached far louder than any well-rehearsed three point sermon. The world expects better from religion, and religion is simply not able to live up to the world's expectations. To be perfectly honest, without the abundance of grace, religion is nothing but a farce!

Are you offended by this incident? It's so easy to take offence. But never forget that offence taking is the clearest evidence of un-grace—putting the offended into the same boat as the offender. Let us not look down in judgement upon this man. No matter how inexcusable his behaviour, he remains a blood bought glorious child of God. He is as much a victim of religion as the rest of us. Fortunately, God has a better way; He calls it "grace!"

We should understand that religion can only help us to suppress our character flaws within limits. Beyond these limits lies our breaking point. That's when our kindly facades drop to expose who we really are—an exposé that is not at all pretty. The plain truth is that rules do not sanctify hearts; hearts can only be sanctified by divine love, and divine love can only be dispensed with great dollops of grace.

The saying that "everybody has a price", usually indicates a price that is sufficiently high enough for a person to dispense with integrity. In the case of politeness and restraint, there is a point beyond which a person's self-restraint cannot help him. This is when deep down animosity is exposed in eruptions of anger. Religion doesn't have the power to deal with the evil in our hearts. All it does is discredit those who practise it, giving critics ample reason to despise Christians. Who can blame them?

Religion is something like a golf pro-shop. We can get ourselves all kitted out in the latest high fashion golfing garb, and buy an expensive set of Tiger Woods endorsed clubs. Although we may look the part, the truth will come out when we tee-up and take our first swing. Out on the fairways, nobody gives a fig about our Tiger Woods outfit. If we ain't got the swing, we ain't got a thing!

Out of the treasure of our hearts our mouths speak[94]. As with botched teeing off; ugly attitudes and so called "righteous" anger, make their way to the surface when challenged by the fairways and sand traps of everyday life.

Like a self-help course, religion tells us what to do to become better people. Conversely, grace tells us what God has done to make us better people. Please don't miss this point—grace bears no resemblance whatsoever to religion! They are not parallel railway tracks going in the same direction. These two tracks run in opposite directions. The one uses fear and manipulation to change our behaviour, while the other accepts our errant behaviour, yet loves us all the same!

The discovery of how enormously God loves us has a way of melting our instinctive defences. Such complete love and acceptance is enough to soften the stoniest of hearts. And softened hearts are loving hearts—they don't have to try to love; true love is spontaneous; gushing over in waves of kindness for no other reason than that they have found personal value in God's love. Uncontrived kind-heartedness and understanding seem to bubble up from within. This happens because love goes to the core of our being. Once our hearts have been captured by His love, our priorities seem to change, not because we try to change, but because love changes us. We are delighted to discover that we are no longer doing the irksome stuff that had plagued us.

Parents tell their children, "God helps those who help themselves". They speak these words as though they are quoting chapter and verse from the Bible. No wonder their children have difficulty coming to grips with grace. Grace is the precise antithesis of this well-worn cliché. Grace is not for those who help themselves; it is for those who have difficulty helping themselves. And if we're honest with ourselves, we cannot deny that we all fall into this sorry group.

From our pulpits we often hear, "Do your best and God will do the rest". Seriously? What about the Gospel of our Lord? Is it not about faith in, and dependence upon a God who understands us; loves us; provides for us; heals us; delivers us; comforts us; supports us; inspires us; teaches us; guides us; encourages us and favours us? As believers, should our first port of call be our limited resources, or our God's limitless resources? Surely we should start with God's almightiness, rather than with human frailties. We are not expected to go it alone until we hit the wall; we are expected to "Walk by faith" 24/7. Faith is not only for getting out of fixes; it is for every moment of living.

"Yes but", I hear some cry, "We are creatures of habit. Our day-to-day routines can be done without bothering God". Really! If that is how we have chosen to live, then how do we differ from the ungodly? God is not an add-on; He is the essence of everything that we are! Although this is true, many sincere believers live as though it is not so.

All believers know that we enter the kingdom by grace alone, without a single good work to our credit. When we entered the kingdom, we expected that the same grace that saved us would keep us saved, but religion convinced us otherwise. Religion relegated us to do whatever we could to hold on for dear life to our "fleeting salvation".

"Doing our best" has become the mantra by which we now live, as though this unbiblical formula has equal standing with 1 Corinthians 15:10. This key scripture states that what I have become has nothing to do with what I have done, but everything to do with what God has done through His grace. Let's settle this once and for all: No amount of self-help can hold our salvation together, nor can it earn us any more of God's love than we already have.

The platitude, "Do your best and God will do the rest" is often given equal standing with God's word. But nothing could be more ungodly than this well-worn cliché. All it does is keep us trying all the harder in the hope that God will add his bit to our bit. But no-one questions why He never adds His bit. Well here's the deal, grace does not need our efforts; grace runs on God's efforts not ours. The only part we play is to receive God's generosity by faith and to share it with others. Sadly, many live by misleading religious clichés, and consequently fail to make withdrawals from His grace.

Something that is surprising about celebrities is that people hang onto their every word, as though they have some cosmic wisdom to impart. There isn't another group of people who have more failed marriages, yet people hang onto every word of advice they offer on marriage. Even though the newspapers are full of their antics, like temper tantrums, spousal abuse, extramarital affairs, illegitimate children, serial marriages, drug addictions, prostitute use etc, people still hold their advice in high regard. If someone is good at play acting, or at playing with a ball, it doesn't necessarily follow that they are good at playing the serious game of life.

Another group of great peddlers of a "better you" are shrinks and therapists. Psychiatrists and psychologists might have the answers for our hag-ups, but seldom have answers for their own. These professionals are among the highest risk occupations out there—they are at greater risk of committing suicide than almost any other profession. It says a lot for psychiatry, doesn't it? Even the great masters, the Sigmund Freud's, with their magnificent records of telling others how life works, failed to figure it out for their own lives, often ending in suicide.

Celebrities, Shrinks, Motivational Speakers and the religious purveyors of flimsy grace have this in common—they are flawed vessels proclaiming a better life—a life that they have not necessarily found for themselves. And it would not be right of us to think that we are any better.

The internet is jam-packed with web sites on fallen telly evangelists and paedophile Catholic priests. Yes, they are God's chosen blood bought vessels, but as with us, they are in desperate need of God's grace. Whether spiritual giants or spiritual infants, no child of God should ever attempt to survive the lure of temptations, without the enablement of God's mercy and grace.

Sadly, when the clergy rule by dominance, it is done at the expense of believers' God given freedom. "Autocracy"; the dominance of one person over another, is forbidden in scripture—bewitchment has no place in God's kingdom!

At the end of the day, the clergy are mere men, as are we, and as such, subject to the same weaknesses. This does not make them lesser beings, it makes them human beings, and their fallibility gives the rest of us reason for hope.

Does God call the clergy into service? Certainly! God works with what He has—a ragtag bunch of flawed saints. Does the gospel reach the world through religion? Most definitely—hidden in all that religiosity is the precious story of God's grace. The fact that God chooses broken vessels to spread the gospel does not reflect poorly on the gospel; rather it demonstrates how far God is prepared to go to reach humanity.

Grace is not selective—if there is grace for the clergy, then the rest of humanity can take heart in knowing that there is grace for their many shortcomings too. Grace is outrageous—long after his death, a sexual philanderer and murderer continues to bless and encourage believers all over the world with his poetry and choral compositions. His name is David—King David!

Despite its obvious flaws, religion's many followers have the privilege of fellowshipping and sharing the word of God with each other. Religion is an imperfect system, as is every other system of this world. Though it may have some virtue, yet it is a gazillion light years short of godliness! Although God's message does reach a dying world through religious channels, religion is not even close to God's idea—it is man's idea! God's idea is "grace!"

When we look at these celebrities and the clergy alike, what does it tell us about ourselves? If the best of the best aren't cutting it, then where does it leave the rest of us? Let's face it, we are all a bunch of scruffs—from the most honoured to the least honoured—none are excluded!

If you cannot put yourself into the category of scruffs, then Christ did not come for you. He came for the lost—the most ragged and bedraggled. It was this class of people that became his nearest and dearest friends, and He didn't try to change them in the least bit—He loved them precisely as they were. It was not words of judgement that elevated these scruffy specimens from bottom feeders to the giddy heights of world changing giants; it was His love that did it! He was a foot washing, burden bearing, crowd feeding, storytelling, authority wielding, lamb cuddling Shepherd. He blended in with every echelon of society. Social outcasts were not too despicable; plebs, not too insignificant, and the socially elite, not too exclusive. He had oodles of time for little children. Never having a single harsh word for His friends—not even when they turned their backs on Him. When He desperately needed their support, they deserted Him like rats escaping a sinking ship. Yet he continued to love them. His compassion shone through His tears, touching hurting humanity in special ways. Lepers were not too filthy for Him, and Pagan Roman Centurions were not too despised for Him. Two thousand years later, His love continues to touch and uplift the trashiest of humanity. Oh how fortunate we are! What a magnificent Saviour we have!

Religion is all about fear and manipulation; grace is all about love and acceptance! Religion says, "I love you if you change"; grace says, "I love you even if you never change." But then again, who can resist surrendering to love? And once surrendered, the potters gentle touch reshapes the way we think—profoundly affecting our outlook on life. With His love, we find it easy to look on the bright side when faced with the most intimidating of circumstances. It is hard to refuse the loving advances of such a true Friend. Behaviour is more responsive to love than to judgement. No wonder God has nothing but love and understanding for the most despicable of us. Jesus was never politically correct, nor was He ever religiously correct—fearlessly saying it like it is! He said that He had not come to judge us but to save us[80]—not something that impressed the religious elite of His day.

This level of love leads one to wonder, "Will the knowledge of such reckless love on God's part result in reckless living on our part? After all, if He has promised to love us regardless, why should we bother restraining ourselves?"

Look at it this way—if your wife were to tell you that she loves you deeply, would you take her unqualified commitment to mean that it is okay to be unfaithful to her? Well of course not! On the contrary, you are likely to respond with even deeper commitment. The same can be said for God's reckless love for you. Contrary to what one would expect; the more one discovers of His gracious love, the less one is inclined to disappoint Him with something as despicable as sin.

A church leader once cautioned me to shield new believers from discovering the freedom of grace until such time as they become mature enough in the faith. He felt that they would not be able to handle liberty wisely. He feared that they would misuse their freedom to fall back into sin.

He could not grasp the fact that such a strategy would be tantamount to committing the felony of fraud. It would leave young converts exposed to the devious tactics of their arch enemy. That crafty snake in the grass takes every opportunity to obstruct the freedom for which Jesus paid so dearly.

Whether well intended or not, in withholding the truth of God's grace from new believers, new believers are defrauded— consigned to a strained relationship with a stern Father. They will forever misunderstand the unconditionality of His love for them. They are left to take on the impossible task of straightening out their lives without the enablement of grace. And without grace's enablement, they are left floundering in sin without the help of God. Sadly, their sincerest strivings are destined to fail, thus consigning their Christian walk to futility. They're unlikely to discover the sanctifying work of the Holy Spirit—He works by grace. But what chance is there that they will ever understand grace? After all, they have been warned to be suspicious of it.

Nothing but graciousness is needed to conquer hardened hearts. Once a heart has been captured by love, it produces loving behaviour without effort. It is God's love; not His judgement that draws people away from iniquitous living. Without grace, believers remain entrapped in their iniquity—weak, vulnerable and powerless to withstand Satan's crafty schemes. When we should be connecting new believers to the power that changes hearts, we connect them to the weakness of their flesh, thus consigning them to an enslavement to dead works. These innocent babes in Christ will never come to understand that nobody's works can sanctify.

Let's settle this once and for all: Dead works are dead works— filthy in the sight of God[135]! If we had introduced new converts to grace from the moment they found Jesus, they would not only have found sanctification, they would have found that they are empowered to walk in obedience. And to top it all, they would have avoided the self-condemnation that comes with shame. There is no getting around it, grace and legalism are not allies—they cannot collaborate. Like the negative fields of two magnets, they repel one another.

Without grace, the best that we can manage is to conceal our guilt and shame by shamming a form of holiness for the sake of religious acceptance. Once bewitched in this way, we become entrapped in guilt; unlikely to grasp the liberating implication of being loved in an entirely unconditional way.

New believers, who innocently begin their Christian walk without knowing the freedom that comes from being unconditionally loved, eventually become adept at acting out a level of "Christian behaviour" that meets with the approval of the group. Sadly, this charade belies what lurks within. Despite this, they become content with their progress, and find comfort in the pious game of religious posturing.

The day that religion elevates us into thinking that we have managed to become something, is the day that we are elevated beyond the reach of grace, and that is a very dangerous place to be. We are all a ragtag bunch of pilgrims, either influenced by religious expectations, or by mercy and grace. Some may be nine tenths scruffian and others eight tenths, but at the end of the day, we are all in the same shabby class, and God has no problem with this. Wherever there are scruffs, you will find Jesus, and wherever you find Jesus, you'll find him loving scruffy individuals. Their scruffiness does not reduce His love for them—to the contrary, the scruffier they are, the more grace He extends to them[128].

Grace cannot accommodate super-spiritual individuals—grace was designed for the poor in spirit. If you are in the super-spiritual class, then the Bible has news for you—God didn't confer religious pomposity upon you—elevated self-importance sounds more like the work of religion than the work of grace.

Grace is not for those who belong to the right spiritual country club where membership is exclusive to those who can afford its snobbery. Grace does not fit into a club that would expect your resignation for infringing its moral code. Grace does not expect anything from you but bedraggleness. And if you can't recognise your bedraggleness, then grace is not for you!

You might be able to say with pride, "Our pastor provides a covering to many ministries" or "We are in fifty countries", or "We have an apostle", or "We don't believe in apostles", or "We are a word of faith church", or "We don't over emphasise faith", and so on ad nauseam. Snobbishness does not cut it with God. Jesus was never exclusive; his closest friends were cursing fishermen, corrupt tax collectors and low life prostitutes. He never had words of accusation or judgement for this raggedy bunch of bedraggled humanity, but He sure had stern words for the religious mob of self-righteous snobs.

In faith's roll of fame, the writer of Hebrews includes a prostitute in his list of faith giants[23]. In Jesus ancestry, there is a prostitute and even worse, a cheat and a murderer[24].

Jesus gave more honour to a prostitute's story than to any other story recorded in the Bible[87]. It was the only story that He said would be retold for as long as the gospel is told. This incident, as recorded by Matthew, was very offensive to the religious mob. It took place in a religious man's home. When a "low life" from the seedy side of town arrived and poured expensive perfume over Jesus, there was a lot of whispering going around the room among the religious elite. "If this was really a man of God, He would know that this was a slut from the under belly of society. How dare He receive her advances so blatantly in front of us without condemning her, or at least expressing His disgust and disapproval?"

Religion is easily offended by what it sees as lesser life; Jesus isn't! Although Jesus was the honoured guest in the house of religious law keepers that day, neither their religiousness, nor their law keeping impressed Him in the least bit. He found more virtue in this outcast of society—a low bred prostitute. In His eyes her value was no less than that of the most upright of respected religious law keepers.

While the religious are offended by the f-words and gutter talk of filthy mouthed humanity, Jesus is loving them! While the religious are having their spiritual sensitivities assaulted by the uncouth; Jesus is loving them! While the religious are being affronted by homosexuality, prostitution and transvestite dressing; Jesus is loving them! While the religious are offended by the abomination of satanic worshipers; Jesus is loving them! He doesn't change them by demanding change—He wins them over with love. Who can resist change when it is inspired by unconditional love? Our strongest resistance is no match for the overwhelming influence of agape love?

If modern religious leaders were present in this religious man's home that day, they too may have demanded, "How can you stoop so low for such filth Jesus? Aren't you supposed to be a member of the triune deity? Isn't there supposed to be a modicum of dignity and decorum in deity?"

Jesus would most likely reply, "If I had to choose between religious dignity and damaged humanity, I would choose damaged humanity every time."

"Why?"

"Because I love them so much that I willingly exchanged my dignity for their shame". Nothing could be more shameful; nothing less dignified; nothing more scandalous; nothing more despised than a person hanging naked on a scorned cross reserved for the worst kind of criminals.

When religion gives up on repeat offenders, Jesus doesn't. He had no harsh words for the motely bunch that followed Him; reserving angry words for religious pretenders!

AUTHORITY GONE TOO FAR

Here is a factual story of religion gone berserk. You don't have to be a theologian to spot the dangers—even an atheist would recognise them. It is easy to dismiss this tragic story as something that only happens to others, but we would do well to take it as a lesson of how not to do church.

Thousands of innocent believers are regularly drawn into cultish subservience. Nobody seems to see the dangers coming. Persuasive leaders abound. Once blind obedience to the authority of church leadership has been established as a "spiritual" imperative, sincere followers desiring to please God will allow themselves to be manipulated, as if God's idea. Before they know it, they are in too deep!

In this story, names of people and churches have been changed for obvious reasons.

I was horrified to see blatant self-promotion of cultic proportions within a church. This church began innocently enough, and appeared to be no different to any other new charismatic church on the block.

Sam Jackson, the founder and leader of Dominion Church, anointed himself bishop. As bishop, he pronounced himself the "spiritual father" of his "spiritual sons", the male members of his congregation.

Hundreds of male members swore their loyalty, obedience and honour to Bishop Sam Jackson in a "Covenant Oath Ceremony". As a mark of their promise, they were issued with covenant rings to be worn at all times. A church document describes this covenant as "a solemn oath of commitment that is binding, enduring, unbreakable, irrevocable and un-dissolvable".

Contained in the document is a section that describes how the "sons" should behave towards their "spiritual father". They pledge always to speak favourably and positively of Bishop, and on formal public occasions, always to acknowledge him and his wife, Sarah first.

Whenever a "son" is publically honoured by society, that son must give credit to his "mentors and role models", Bishop and Mrs Jackson.

Any approaches to Bishop must be respectful and honourable because "he is the tangible expression of God". They are instructed that it is better to offend others than to offend him.

They must feel Bishop's flow and be attentive to his thoughts and directions, because this gives unity and power to what God is saying and doing through him. They must endorse and fully support whatever Bishop Jackson endorses, and promote whatever he promotes. They are not permitted to speak or gesture while Bishop Jackson is talking. "Sons" are not permitted to openly disagree or become familiar with him in front of others.

When the bishop and his wife enter a room, they must rise in honour and acknowledgement. They may not take their seats before the Jacksons are seated. When dining with the Jacksons, they may not eat until the Jacksons begin eating.

"Sons" are encouraged to sit close to the pulpit; to be vocal during his preaching; agreeing with what he says with "amen" and "that's right"; clapping; shouting and laughing when appropriate.

They are told to take notes of bishop's sermons to demonstrate how highly they value the Word of God from him.

They should always be dressed well at Bishop's meetings. They are required to look happy, smile, be friendly and encouraging.

They must demonstrate Bishop's importance by travelling and supporting him when he speaks elsewhere.

They are not to tolerate anyone speaking critically of Bishop, his wife, their family or the church.

They should celebrate Bishop's special occasions with surprises on birthdays, anniversaries and special achievements as a sign of love, honour and respect for him.

"Sons" must be prepared to defend any problems arising out of Bishop's mistakes and never expose his weaknesses.

Nauseating, isn't it?

In requiring its men to swear an oath of loyalty and obedience to Sam Jackson, Dominion Church has transformed itself from a church into a cult. A cult is a religious devotion directed towards a particular figure who imposes excessive control over members.

It is particularly disturbing when hundreds of men are deceived into swearing a lifetime obligation to a mere fallible mortal.

While honour, loyalty and obedience are admirable dispositions, the moment they become compulsory, they lose their virtue. To impose them under oath, smacks of religious blackmail!

Strangely, no mention is made of the women of the church, apart from Bishop Jackson's wife, known as Pastor Sarah. One assumes that wives are to fall in with their husband's whims and fancies and do what they are told.

The religious totalitarianism that is practiced there is not unique. While not blatantly formalised into covenant oaths; it is nevertheless an unspoken practice in many suburban churches. It is true to say that churches are not meant to be democracies, but by the same token, neither are they meant to be autocratic dictatorships.

The misuse of pastoral authority to exploit followers, requiring them to swear an oath of loyalty, is unbiblical. Scripture offers neither precedent nor mandate for dictatorial manipulation; in fact scripture stands firmly against it.

Certainly we should support one another, including our pastor, but in no way should our support extend to blind obedience and blind loyalty to any man—total submission belongs to Christ alone!

A pastor's role is that of a humble servant/leader, ordained to serve God's children; not to heavy-handedly oppress, coerce and tyrannize them. He is not called to an exalted dictatorial position of despotism; he is called to the humble position of sheep feeding servant-hood. Pastors are not leaders who serve. On the contrary, they are servers who lead—two vastly different approaches that bear no resemblance to each other.

The practice of signing, or for that matter even verbally affirming some sort of "covenant" whereby compliant supporters pledge their subservient loyalty to one leader for the rest of their lives, regardless of where he may lead them, is enormously risky and spiritually dangerous. This kind of all-inclusive binding covenant provides no escape clauses. When the leader is misled, they are all misled, when he falls, they all fall.

When religion misuses its authority to control, it is flirting with cultism. This kind of manipulative religiosity provides the perfect platform for tragic outcomes. Beware of religion when it becomes manipulative, for in its cauldron boils a witch's brew of devilish bondage!

Religion is not too different to cultism—often teetering on the brink of witchcraft. In many cases, another tiny degree of control is enough to push it over the edge. When this happens, it happens without fanfare—it is so subtle that it's coming about usually goes by unnoticed—church services continue as usual, and nobody is any the wiser. No alarm bells are sounded—innocent believers are simply ensnared without realising that they have slipped over the edge. Think twice! History is littered with cultism's tragic outcomes.

There is trouble brewing for the members of Dominion Church—it is time for them to be afraid!

Entering into covenant with a man should be approached with extreme caution—it is a lifetime commitment that can never be reversed. We are not even expected to make a covenant with God. If we do, we are effectively saying that the New Covenant is deficient and in need of amendment.

God cannot afford to have an unreliable covenant, and humanity is not reliable enough to keep its end of the deal. When God makes a covenant, He makes it robust enough to survive humanity's fallibility.

History has proved that the best of mankind has a breaking point. Peter reached his, denying that he even knew his dearest Friend, Jesus, at a time when Jesus needed him most[25].

There is no need for us to make any further covenants with God. He has already found a reliable party in the person of Jesus to do it for us. For God's covenant of grace to be unshakable, it requires unquestionable integrity from all parties to the agreement. Of course, that's no problem for God, but humanity's defective integrity is skewed with self-interest and hidden agendas. Mankind's flawed history is a sorry tale, strewn with broken promises. Humanity simply cannot be trusted with the responsibility of staying in covenant with God. On the other hand, the God/man, Jesus, has no problem with integrity. He has taken man's responsibility upon His shoulders—we can rest assured that He is well able to take care of our side of the covenant without our help, or more correctly, our hindrance.

SUPER SPIRITUAL DOESN'T SUIT YOU

We are all children of God. The most mature admission for any believer to make is, "I am a child." Sounds like an oxymoron, doesn't it? But when it comes to God's measure, those who consider themselves to be mature might be surprised to discover just how much more growing up lies ahead. We may be at different levels of childhood, but every last one of us is no more than a "child" of God.

God loves His kids. Isabella, my two month old granddaughter isn't much of a talker yet. So far she can say two words, "Ngoooo" and "Ngaaaa". That's all she needs to say to climb right into her grandpa's heart. God is not expecting grandiose prayers from us—we can capture His heart with a few poorly chosen words of affection— the kind of words that would leave the prim and proper thoroughly unimpressed, and possibly even offended by the familiarity of soppy love talk.

Sometimes when Kyle, my two year old grandson is tired and out of sorts, he lets us know about his irritation in no uncertain terms. As miserable as he can be, my love for him never skips a beat. At our absolute worst behaviour, God's heart continues to pump pure love for us.

Then when this little guy interrupts me in my study while I am busy writing, I can't resist his little mischievous smile. I stop typing midsentence to chase him around the room on all fours. I love hearing his little squeals of delight. God is never too busy to join in with our laughter—He will drop anything He is doing just to participate in our pleasures, no matter how immature our games may be.

Now Dylan, my eleven year old grandson is a lot more mature, but he is still a kid. I live just to hear what he told me that special day when the two of us built a small paper hot air balloon, "Grandpa! Grandpa! You are the best grandpa in the whole wide world!" God cherishes our words when we say, "Daddy! Daddy! You are the best daddy in the whole wide universe!" I can just see his heart skip a beat, as mine did that special day.

Religion may expect us to stand on ceremony with the right introduction, solemnness and respectful protocol in God's holy presence, but God our Father expects nothing more than our childish gibberish and gooble-dee-gook. He wants our company and He is quite happy to take all the immaturity that goes with it. Not even our childish tantrums and silly nonsense faze Him. We are his kids—He understands us and loves us dearly!

My grandchildren would insult me if they were to stand on ceremony in my company as religion requires of its followers. How can we possibly impress a Dad with our religiously invented rights and rituals—we are His kids and He is our Papa. Worse still, how dare we come to Him with our religious epilates of Christian rank proudly displayed upon our shoulders, or our medals of Christian achievements upon our chests—the kind that gives us superiority in the company of fellow believers? We may impress the congregation with our boast of a Doctorate of divinity, or with church rank and years of selfless service, but will a God who simply wants His kids to know Him as Papa be impressed? Personal elevation may go down well with compatriots in pews, but at the end of the day, God doesn't address us as doctor, pastor or prophet. Is He impressed with our exaggerated self-aggrandisement? I don't think so!

In spite of what Jesus had to say on the subject, religion insists on conferring rank upon leadership. If Jesus' description of greatness is to be taken seriously, then levels of hierarchy ought to work in reverse. The most senior would be servant to the most junior. The highest rank would be a servant to the most immature church member[19]. Religious rank is easily explained away—tritely ascribing it to a function; not a rank. Yet, all too often in practice, the big chief casts a long shadow.

The institutionalised structure of churches is often no different to the structure of a business. The higher up the ladder, the bigger the stick. In business, the head honcho has the power to hire and fire anybody in the corporation, and his vision becomes everybody's vision. Sounds familiar, doesn't it? Jesus' injunction, that anyone aspiring to be first must become a servant to everybody else, seems not to apply to religious hierachy[19]. Yet congregants are expected to live by it.

Upon Brian and Jane joining a church, the senior pastor took great pains over explaining how their church differed from most other churches in so far as leadership goes. As he explained, most churches have a triangular shaped leadership hierarchy with the senior pastor at the top of the triangle. In the case of their church, the triangle did not stand upright; it lay flat on its face, making all members and pastors equal.

Brian was thrilled to hear this. But alas! It didn't take too long to see through this deception—with time the pastor's heavy handedness became all too evident. He had the power to fire members on a whim; to forbid them reading certain books; to forbid business relationships with certain individuals; to cause the cancelation of business deals and to forbid friendship with people that he had blackballed. Besides having this degree of control over the minds of his congregants, he attempted to continue controlling Brian and Jane even after he had given them their marching orders.

The line that divides religion from cultism is so fine that it is often difficult to tell on which side of the line religion actually stands. In giving humanity a free will, God chose not to control anybody. Free will is free will! If the mighty Emperor of the entire universe is gracious enough to allow mere mortals to choose, then it is incumbent upon us to emulate Him and allow others the same freedom. Church leaders who don't see it this way, continue to reign by totalitarianism.

It leaves one to wonder whose mandate they are carrying out. Makes one think, doesn't it? If any leader has given himself the right to control anybody, then it is obvious that that leader has crossed the line and fallen into the sewer of cultism. When this happens, it is time for the congregation to be afraid!

This church's ways are not unique. Jesus said that we should be on the lookout for wolves in sheep's clothing. Yes, "discipling" is ordained by Jesus for the benefit of the flock. But all too often, it is misused to frighten believers into "toeing the company line". How on earth did heavy-handedness find its way into a kingdom that is characterised by servant-hood? This is not the way of Jesus—He described Himself as a servant. Sadly, un-Christ-like domineering is an accepted practice in many churches. Often leadership has no compunction about overriding the very freedom that Jesus obtained for all. Little regard is given to the liberty embedded in the glorious gospel of our Lord! There are leaders who will do whatever it takes to hang onto "divinely unsanctioned" authority. Sad as it is to say, religious bullying is commonplace in many churches!

"Fathering" in the gentle way that Jesus fathered is wonderful, but fathering in a controlling sense is diabolical. When the accountability and love connection between believers and their heavenly Father is replaced with a connection to an earthly father, it should be obvious that we have strayed from the New Covenant—it is a covenant of grace! When Jesus foresaw this kind of misuse of power, He said that we are not to call anybody our "father". Other than our biological father, that term is reserved exclusively for our heavenly Father[27].

Despite such a clear instruction, "fathering" in the kingdom is often no more than an opportunity to impose control. Once believers have been persuaded to accept that fathering is God's idea, they willingly surrender their God given dominium, exchanging it for subservience to the religious elite. Sadly, this subtle deception side-lines grace, and side-lined grace is side-lined Jesus! Although every saint is fully empowered with dominion, sadly, few walk in the authority of it.

This leads straight into the hands of another power junky. Guess who is standing in the wings waiting to pounce on believers stripped of their authority?

Three notable Bible teachers and strong proponents of "fathering" also known as "shepherding" and "discipleship", Charles Simpson, Derek Prince and Bob Mumford, later publicly distanced themselves from these practices. Derek Prince withdrew in 1983, stating his belief that "We were guilty of the Galatian error: Having begun in the Spirit, we quickly degenerated into the flesh." Bob Mumford issued a formal repentance statement to the Body of Christ in 1990, and was quoted as saying, "Discipleship was wrong. I repent. I ask forgiveness."

Despite these distinguished leaders' unequivocal recant of these false doctrines, many of their dedicated followers throughout the world have doggedly held onto them. They simply ignore the fact that they were repudiated by their mentors, and conveniently continue to mismanage and misgovern by religious strong arm practices in the guise of discipleship. For power junkies, it is more expedient to empower themselves with these flawed principles, than to admit that they are erroneous. Error or not, they lend so-called "god endorsed legitimacy" to the ungodly practise of religious manipulation.

Power is beguiling—once empowered, it is not something that can easily be surrendered, especially when it affords unusual privileges to those in power. History has shown that political power is intoxicating—likely to continue until the one in power is deposed. The misuse of power is a church split in the making. Be careful—church splits are painful. It is better to walk away with love in your heart, than to participate in the acrimony and bitterness that goes with church splits—there are never any winners!

When only one person's vision is permitted, then everybody else's vision must be sacrificed. It is done in the cause of submitting to "God's appointed man". Ever wondered why the church has so many square pegs in round holes? Wonder no more! While not necessarily said in so many words, there is nevertheless a subtle pressure on members to volunteer for church duties, even if they have no aptitude for the assigned tasks.

I know a pastor who takes a very different view to this. He asks each member what their particular vision is, and then asks them how the church can assist to make their vision a reality. In this way, every member is doing what he or she has been called by God to do. Each member's gifting is given every opportunity to blossom in a natural way. Nobody ends up trying to do something for which they have neither aptitude nor passion.

Yes, the church needs a common goal and vision, but if the common goal and vision cannot accommodate the various divine callings of each individual, then it ends up with a gathering of misfits.

Very often the practise of running roughshod over individual congregants' visions, goals and aspirations, makes spectators instead of participants of them. When they do not have a heart for the assigned task, they simply end up suppressing their God given mission and dutifully drift aimlessly through the motions of nominal church attendance. Is it any wonder that 90% of church work is performed by 10% of the congregation?

This chapter is not meant to be pastor bashing; it is meant to challenge the validity of religious steamrolling. Pastors are no different to the rest of us, and just as susceptible to religious entrapment. Church office is not church rank, neither is it institutionalised dictatorship!

How do we discern the difference between rank and office? "Office" is an anointing for the purpose of liberating and empowering believers. "Rank" is different—far removed from anointing! Where rank exists, believers are at risk of being disempowered by an elite class of believer. Sadly, history has shown that the clergy has often empowered themselves by disempowering sincere believers. Once an ecclesiastical pecking order has been established, commendable tasks such as "fathering" and "discipling" transform into manipulation and control. Steamrolling, its stock in trade!

Confusion arises when anointed leaders deviate from Jesus' model. When leadership is no longer a matter sheep feeding servant-hood, it is time for the congregation to be afraid! When leadership exalts itself into the realm of dictatorship, it is time to run! Religion is beguiling—before one knows it, one is integrated into its hierarchical structures. Leaders are not usually aware that they have deviated from the purity of grace—they are innocently caught up in the whirlwind of performing for God.

"If you welcome a prophet as one who speaks for God, you will receive the same reward a prophet gets." [60] It is incumbent upon us to give honour where honour is due; not where honour is demanded!

Jesus never called Himself Pastor Jesus, and Elijah did not call himself Prophet Elijah, yet modern day leaders have no compunction about conferring lofty titles upon themselves.

If our pastors don't understand the error of self-aggrandisement, it is not time for us to straighten them out. In as much as we are anointed, so are they. We dare not touch God's anointed with criticism[22]. The most that we can do is to love and support them. Either they discover grace for themselves, or they don't discover it at all. It's not between us and them; it's between them and their heavenly Father.

According to Jesus, John the Baptist was greater than all the prophets, yet Jesus said that John was not as great as one who is least in the kingdom[90]. Who is least in the kingdom? You are in the kingdom, and if you see yourself as the weakest kind of believer, you are greater than John the Baptist, Elijah and any of the Old Testament prophets and kings, including David, the man after God's own heart.

Why has Jesus given you such lofty status? The answer is clear: None of the Old Testament saints had the privilege of being born-again. The blood of Jesus had not yet been spilt to make rebirth possible. Old Testament believers used the blood of lambs as an interim measure until such time as Jesus, the Lamb of God, would ultimately be slain for them.

When Jesus died, He first went to hell to retrieve Adam's lost dominion for our sakes, and then proceeded to paradise where Old Testament saints were held captive[91]. There He preached the gospel of grace and allowed them to decide for themselves to either accept or reject His plan of redemption. They were given the same choice that we were given. In order to be released from captivity, they had to receive Jesus' wonderful sacrifice for themselves. As with us, even Old Testament saints could only be saved by grace. In the same way that our good works could not do it for us; their good works could not do it for them. Only after their individual decisions to accept God's redemptive plan of grace, could Jesus lead these captives into the captivity of heaven. It took the same grace that saved us to save them.

It is interesting to note that the Pope was not always so lavishly attired, and he didn't always live as royalty in a palace of grandiose proportions and stupendous opulence—the envy of the world's heads of state.

Before the reign of Roman Emperor Constantine, the Pope was a pauper and a fugitive on the run. There was a price on his head. He certainly wasn't an illustrious religious figure. It was only when Constantine adopted Christianity as Rome's official religion that he exalted the Pope to share equal status with himself. He decided that the Pope should sit on a throne, wear a crown, be as lavishly enrobed as any king, and reside in an opulent palace. He also decided that he should be honoured with the grandest of pomp and ceremony. This was the Emperor's idea; not God's.

God is thoroughly unimpressed with our self-promotion. I was once asked to film the birthday party of the senior pastor of the largest, most prosperous congregation in town. The catering was top class. The guest list, impressive—the who's who of religious achievers. Among the dignitaries were pastors from other congregations. Self-acclamation was obvious. I couldn't help feeling a sense of sympathy for the small time pastors whose little congregations would never be able to entertain on such a lavish scale. They would most likely count themselves fortunate if they were to get a homemade cake from a widow as the only acknowledgement of their birthdays. Were these poor pastors really impressed with such immodest extravagance? Or did they see through it and recognise it for what it was?

JUSTICE OR GRACE?

"Don't forget that God is not only gracious, He is also just." Anybody who has chosen grace in preference to religion will have had to contend with this well-meant adage. One can be excused for thinking that justice poses a challenge to grace. After all, if justice and grace are so opposite, how is it possible for God to be both "just" and "gracious" at the same time?

"If God is love, how come He sends people to Hell?" is a jibe that often pops up in the form of a facetious objection from unbelievers. Facetious or not, one can be forgiven for perceiving that it poses a challenge to the concept of grace. I believe that reasonable questions deserve reasonable answers.

A dishonest person always leaves himself open to the possibility of being found out. Some push the envelope so far that one can only wonder how they manage to get any sleep at all. One would think that the terror of being found out and brought to justice would keep them awake. God is holy—His honesty is flawless—He doesn't lose any sleep wondering if He'll be found out (of course, in reality, we know He never slumbers nor sleeps, but there is nothing in His past to keep Him awake). We can rest assured—His faultless holiness guarantees

His eternal position as invincible emperor of the entire universe. He has no moral weaknesses, and therefore cannot be overthrown.

At the very core of holiness is justice—you cannot have the one without the other. God is a just God because He is holy and He is holy because He is just. If God were not to insist on justice, He would no longer be holy and that would make His position as ruler of the universe tenuous at best.

Because God's holiness is upheld by His justice, He simply cannot allow injustice to go unchecked—it must be remedied with an appropriate measure of justice. Hell exists because holiness requires justice to be served.

You may want grace without justice from God, but that is asking for something that is simply not possible—God would have to become unjust to make an exception for you, and we can be quite certain that that will never happen.

You may prefer grace to justice, until a heinous crime is perpetrated against you, and then suddenly justice becomes more important to you than grace. Think of it this way: You are waiting with your best man and a full church of wedding guests for your bride to arrive. She doesn't arrive. Then someone rushes into the church with the news. Your bride has been car-jacked on her way to church, and has been severely beaten up and gang raped. Her beautiful face has been smashed and permanently disfigured.

You, being a gracious man, have a choice to either demand justice and press charges against these monstrous thugs, or graciously let them off the hook to continue their rampage of terror. What is your choice?

"Justice!" I hear you demand with indignation. And we all stand together with you in complete agreement. Suddenly justice is better than grace. A just God must demand justice before grace, otherwise He is done for. So hell must exist as a place where justice can be meted out in order to uphold holiness.

You and I must be brought to book for our sins, and the penalty has to be a hellish eternal death. Here is the quandary: God being a loving God does not want to see you judged and condemned. But in order for holiness to prevail, justice must be allowed to run its course—He has no choice—rectification is required, and that takes justice.

Here is where His love for us exceeds His demand for justice. Hell is the last place He wants for us—He loves us so much that He is willing to allow someone else to take the fall for us. To do this, He had to find a human being without sin. If he had any sin of his own, he would have to go to hell anyway. Here is the dilemma: We all know that such a person has never existed nor ever will. Foreseeing this predicament, God came up with a brilliant master plan to save humanity from the punishment it so rightly deserved. His one and only Son would become a human being, live on planet earth, be put to a painful death, and go to hell in our place. It takes a whole heap of grace to go that far, wouldn't you say? Can there be any doubt that we are dearly loved?

Fortunately Jesus, His Son, could not be held in hell indefinitely—He had no personal sin to keep Him there.

In a supreme act of love, His grace triumphed over justice, paving the way for us to escape hell and gain heaven.

Going to heaven one day is something to look forward to, but heaven is only the spinoff of something else of great value. What could possibly be as valuable as heaven? A personal relationship with our heavenly Father is the greatest prize of all. A caring friendship with our loving Dad is as good as life gets—with Him at our side, we will never be alone.

Although, in an act of supreme love for us, His Son paid the ultimate price for our clemency, yet we still have the choice of either accepting clemency as a free gift, or foolishly insist on paying for our own sins. The choice is ours—it's a no brainer! If you haven't done it yet, why wait? You can do it right now. Just pray, "Dear God, I am a sinner—I turn to you in repentance. Jesus, thank you for dying in my stead. I accept the gift of your righteousness in exchange for my sin. Make me your child. Holy Spirit, please show me the way."

If this is the first time that you have prayed a prayer like this; God has just become your Father—you have been reborn into His family. I would love to help you understand what has just happened to you and answer any questions you may have. Please feel free to blog me.

We cannot blame people for not wanting to get too close to God. Religion has portrayed Him as holy and unapproachable while there is sin in our lives. The truth of the matter is that we all have sin in our lives when compared to Jesus. Although preachers often tell of His graciousness, some feel compelled to balance it with a list of do's and don't s. Sadly, this is all it takes to set sincere believers off on a wild goose chase—the futile quest of performing for God's approval—a sure way to miss grace altogether.

Whether religion is responsible for it or not, many believe God to be an omnipotent thug who beats us into submission with all kinds of catastrophes and misfortunes. They see Him as an authoritarian school master who makes the school of life a place of torture and terror. To them He is stiff, strict and severe—using rigid archaic laws and curses to bully us into submission.

Another way that Christ is often portrayed is as a feeble effeminate wimp. Some statues depict an anaemic weakling hanging on a cross. No wonder men often view God and religion as something for women and wimps. They don't understand that He was in the tough trade of carpentry considerably longer than His three short years in ministry. In His day, there weren't electric bench saws and the like to make carpentry easy; He did everything the hard way. Jesus was as tough as nails, with calloused hands and rock solid biceps—every inch a man's man!

With His masculinity being misrepresented as wimpishness, and His Father's loving character being misrepresented as holy thuggery, it is no wonder that mankind has come to form a horribly distorted picture of who He actually is. With so much misinformation out there, it's not surprising that religion is a subject to be avoided at all costs, especially at dinner parties.

As long as we believe all these distortions, we won't see Him as our Father, defender, friend, physician and provider. What's really cool about God, is that He loves us just as we are, and if we never change, He will continue to love us all the same. I must warn you though! Just knowing that you are so deeply loved is life changing in and of itself.

Sanctification does not target our actions; it targets our hearts. We might as well resign ourselves to the fact that our efforts to live right do not bring about meaningful and lasting change. For it to be genuine and lasting, it must start with our hearts. Once our hearts and thoughts have been captured by His love, it is only a matter of time before our actions follow suit.

God's way of loving us into holiness is a whole lot smarter than religion's way. Sheer grit and determination do not deal with the way we intuitively think. Unless change takes place at heart level, we don't have holiness; we have charm! When our actions say one thing, while our hearts say the opposite, we are practicing hypocrisy. It takes love of the unconditional kind to make a difference at heart level. The wonderful truth about His love is that it has a way of turning the stoniest of hearts into mush.

We serve the God we have come to imagine Him to be. If we get our perception of Him wrong, we end up relating to someone who isn't remotely like the God of the Bible. If we picture Him to be rigid, stern and foreboding, we will live in a relationship ruled by dread and fear, and not find it easy to enter His presence joyfully. But when our concept of His character lines up with His grace, our actions are ruled by love.

A person infused with God's love can do no harm. His love solves the sin problem—something that legalism simply cannot do. We don't hurt people we love. Nor can we covet, envy, lie, commit adultery or steal from them while loving them.

Sure God is just! But He is also infinitely loving, unconditionally forgiving, compassionate, encouraging, and immensely kind! We can relax in the tranquillity of an undemanding relationship marked with acceptance, love, peace and hope. His presence is not a place of foreboding and dread; it is a place of peace, joyfulness and pleasure[46].

What a joy it is to honour our God. Religion will help us to do this with all kinds of religious activities. But beware! Even something as beautiful as praise and worship can regress into something that is mechanical, religious and ritualistic. Don't get me wrong—I am not singling out traditional churches; I am referring to all churches. Sadly, with the passing of time, vibrant divine romance has a tendency of sliding into tiresome rituals.

Rather than all our breathless running about for brownie points, there is a better way to honour God. It's just resting and luxuriating contentedly in the pleasure of knowing that we are unconditionally loved.

How can we be so sure that resting in His presence is more honouring to Him than all sorts of hectic churchified hubbub? While Jesus was visiting His friends, the one sister was frantically preparing lunch for Him while the other was just restfully absorbing His love[28]. The frantic one complained to Jesus that her sister had left her to do all the chores. Jesus was quick to point out, "Only one thing is necessary", and that one thing is not being busy for Jesus; it is merely resting calmly in His love.

Isn't Jesus' approach to our relationship just so refreshing? Busting blood vessels for Jesus doesn't earn brownie points. He prefers hanging out with His best mates. What could be better than being with a friend? Especially with a friend who sticks closer than a brother. Where there is love, there is trust, and where there is trust, there is rest—nothing could be more peaceful—nothing more inspirational!

We get everything for simply resting in His love. But we really mess up badly when we start adding this and that to what is already a perfect relationship. Like a painting of an idyllic little desert island with two or three palm trees leaning outwards, surrounded by calm turquoise waters and a few fluffy white clouds. The painting is complete—no more brush strokes are necessary to evoke a relaxed sense of peace and tranquillity. Then the painter adds a rust bucket oil tanker, belching black smoke to the background. Suddenly all sense of serenity is lost.

It is the same with grace. We must accept grace for what it is— free and undeserved, and not try to improve upon it with all kinds of churchified buzzing about. The best vintage must be taken straight!

ENTITLEMENT

We work for a living. Our emoluments are in direct proportion to our efforts. The more time spent at the rock face, the more we are entitled to collect from the paymaster. It's how we bring home the bacon. This is the way of the world, but is it the way of the Kingdom?

Remuneration is the reason that we are prepared to trade our leisure time for a hard day's schlep. We wouldn't put ourselves through the grind of sanity destroying pressure at the salt mine, if it wasn't for pay day. There has to be a reward—something in it for us to keep us coming back day after day, year in and year out. You get nothing for nothing; or so they say.

Religion requires the same work ethic. If we want something from God, we need to put in the slog. Deuteronomy 28 clearly outlines the effort required to release the blessings. We are to do "all" seven hundred and something laws without exception, in order to gain the good stuff. One slipup ruins all of our efforts, and cancels all our blessings—worse still, we end up getting cursed for the slightest underperformance. It doesn't have to be something evil—even something as innocent as wearing a suit consisting of a combination of fibres, like wool and cotton, make us law breakers[104]. Those who claim to keep the law are only kidding themselves—nobody in the entire history of mankind has ever managed to do it.

According to Jesus, even our thought life makes us law breakers[29]. That pretty well seals it, doesn't it? We are disqualified on the basis of our musings! The bottom line is: We are simply not capable of fulfilling the necessary conditions for unlocking Deuteronomy's blessings; period!

Let's face it. We have tried it all before, and for one reason or another, got tired, and the project faded, ultimately slipping off our radar screens. After a while, we gathered enough gumption to give it another shot, but that didn't last too long either.

Any thought of gaining the blessings through law keeping is simply a delusion—it serves only to keep us out of the blessings. Besides, do we really think that God has to be obligated into doing something that He has already decided to do for us?

We have come to believe that, when we have behaved well and done a good deed here and there, we have a bargaining chip—something to trade for blessings at God's convenience store in the sky.

In the first place, before we go hammer and tongs for these rewards, we ought to make sure that we know how these blessings are released. Don't lose sight of the fact that we do not live in the dispensation of the law; we live in the dispensation of grace. The Old Covenant was a "rewards for work done" covenant, while the New Covenant is a testamentary bequest of "grace and favour". Inheritances are gifts, and gifts cannot be earned; they can only be received without payment. That being the case, how do we take ownership of the gifts bequeathed to us? Here is the conundrum: Nothing is free of charge. Fortunately, it is not we that must earn them; Jesus has already earned them for us, and therefore, they are unequivocally ours. Isn't it wonderful? He did the work, thereby gaining legal ownership. And that's not where the story ends. Thereafter He conferred ownership upon us by way of His Last Will and Testament. On His death, we became co-heirs together with Him[117]. Since He died and rose from the dead, everything He owns, we own! If we are not making use of our inheritances, then it is plain—we don't know that we are beneficiaries, and consequently, do not claim ownership of what is legally ours. Some know that they have inherited, but don't know what they have inherited. Seeing that we have inherited so much, there is nothing further to be earned. Our only responsibility is to appropriate that which is legally ours. We do this by declaring ownership by faith. Grace is not an extension of the Old Covenant; it is a whole different ball game—diametrically opposite to the system of allocating blessings and curses in direct response to our actions.

Salvation includes a whole lot more than being saved from the fires of hell—we need to be saved out of all sorts of predicaments like sicknesses, broken relationships and lack. Every so often, we all experience one sort of bankruptcy or another. Fortunately, there is more than enough grace to go around.

Let's settle this once and for all! None of God's salvation can be bought on the labour market—nothing about God's favour and grace can be earned. Grace does not allow for bargaining with God as in a game of monopoly where we can trade airports and train stations for real estate and hotels. In one fell swoop, Jesus ended the practice of one favour exchanged for another. A favour for a favour belongs to the shady underworld of the Mafioso.

Our piffling deeds do not entitle us to haggle with God. Everything we get from Him comes via unearned, unmerited, undeserved gratuitous bequest. Come and help yourself to whatever you desire[103]. Just bring the right currency. Everything is available. Beware though! The currency of good works is not legal tender in the kingdom. The one and only acceptable currency is "faith". Exchange it for blessings. The shelves are fully stocked with every blessing listed in Deuteronomy 28. The word "whatever" is a pretty all-inclusive word, wouldn't you say? It's the word Jesus used when He said, "Whatever you ask the Father in My name He will give you"[103]. NKJV Whenever Jesus says something, you can take Him at His word.

You decide what you want—your wildest imagination is never too outlandish—availability always exceeds demand. The bigger your basket, the bigger your blessings. While God is the supplier, there will never be a supply crisis—His resources are infinite and therefore inexhaustible! Be sure not to sell yourself short!

When we are not living to gain God's love, but rather living in His love, life takes on a whole new meaning, and our lives turn out a whole lot different. Our relationship has nothing to do with trying to get Him to love us—that's something He has already decided on.

There is a huge difference between frenzied striving for, and peacefully resting in. The Bible talks about entering His Sabbath rest permanently[30]. The Sabbath rest is no longer a holiday that comes around once a week; it is a permanent retirement from anything that smacks of religious striving—a 24/7 state of rest! A place of rest is a place of relaxing, and we are not relaxed when we are frantically trying to impress God. Our frenzied flapping about to gain His approval is exactly what prevents us from luxuriating in the serenity of His peace. In the tranquillity of His presence we rest, soaking in His love, favour and grace without cost. Privileges abound—nothing is in short supply!

A promise is a promise, and God's promises are not what we strive to get; it's what we rest in—that's what's meant by trust. What more is there to be done? The answer to this question should be obvious. Nothing we can possibly do can improve upon what Jesus achieved for us on the cross.

Knowledge of such freely available grace, should not lead us to believe in fatalism. Fatalism says that we have no way of steering events in our lives—whatever is meant to be will be. As with Doris Day's number one hit in the 50's, "Que sera sera, Whatever will be will be". If it were so, Jesus would not have told us to ask, seek and knock[9]. Prayer, vision, desire and passion steer our lives in the direction of our choices. He gave us dominion over the earth, and He allows us the freedom to make both good and bad choices.

Let's face it, mere mortals cannot obligate Almighty God to do anything. But the good news is, He has already obligated Himself by covenant to do anything we ask. He decided that Jesus would take the curse of the law upon Himself so that it would not fall upon us[3]. Jesus fulfilled the law for us, so that we would not have to do it ourselves[2]. He has cleared the way for us to have a relationship with Him uncluttered by sin—not because we don't sin, but because our sins have already been atoned for. It happened two thousand years ago—all sin was atoned for—even the ones yet to be committed[132].

More than that, He didn't just deal with our sins, He dealt with the entire sin issue[64]. No longer is any record permitted to be kept of our sins in heaven[82]. That doesn't mean that we shouldn't repent of our sins. Sin is the human race's most terrifying foe. Although we are forgiven in advance, we still have to live with the awful outcomes of our unfortunate choices.

If I have made my best friend's wife pregnant, God forgives me, but my friend's wife remains pregnant, and I will have to contend with my friend's wrath, my wife's fury, loss of my children's respect, an expensive divorce that may drive me to the brink of bankruptcy, a complicated fathering of an illegitimate child, and the loss of trust of loved ones. The list of unfortunate consequences is endless. This is a lifetime penalty in exchange for a moment's indiscretion—a brief encounter with pleasure in exchange for an expensive embarrassment that just won't go away.

With grace there is no need to depend upon something as unreliable as our resolve to live right. We have something a great deal more dependable than that—so dependable that it can be taken to the bank. It is our God imputed righteousness—it never wanes or fluctuates, not even when we foolishly fall into sin[132]. With it, there are no more maybe's, if's or but's. What Jesus has already done for us is unquestionably certain.

Jesus had the time of day for sinners, never judging them. He surrounded himself with the unsavoury outcasts of society. Yet there is not a single mention of Him ever judging them. Yes, He instructed a sinner not to sin, but before doing so, He first made it perfectly clear that He was not judging Her[105]. The truth is that He didn't come to judge the world, but to save it—a difficult pill for pharisaic Christians to swallow[80].

Much to the religious elite's disgust, Jesus was the friend of sinners, and He still is. He was perfectly comfortable to be with the dregs of society, and He still is. But He was decidedly uncomfortable with pretenders, and He still is. Sadly, legalism would make pretenders of us all if we were to give it half a chance to mesmerise us under its spooky spell.

Let us never forget who we are. Pretending is not only distasteful to Jesus; it is also distasteful to unbelievers who have to put up with our sanctimonious pretensions. How nauseating to meet a "perfect Christian"—a Mr Goody-two-shoes. He is the one who would avoid the company of cursing and swearing, yet think nothing of betraying a confidence. To know a man is not to know what he says; it is to know what goes on in the depths of his heart.

While we may think that we are somebody, let us not forget that, no matter how well we wear our halos, they are always slightly askew. Even though we may not acknowledge it ourselves, others can't miss it. Sometimes Christianity can become a matter of keeping up with the saintly Jones'. We may be able to hold our own in Christian company as we pepper our conversations with churchified clichés in the language of "Christianese", but we still have to adjust our slipping halos—they keep drifting off to the side. It's not the cocked halos that are the problem; we all have cocked halos; it's pretending that they are sitting straight that is the problem!

Pretending is for little girls playing housie housie—not a game that believers should be bothering with. We are all a bunch of bedragglers. Let's not pretend to be anything else. Jesus came for the bedraggled—our pious pretending does not impress Him in the least bit.

There is nothing more loathsome than the pretence of piety, and there is nothing more attractive than the honesty of a bedraggled follower of Jesus, whose only claim to fame is that he is loved by His Heavenly Dad. Though we may not be prepared to admit it, we all fall into the same shabby class of ragtag believers.

Our secret church achievements may be unknown to many, but oh how satisfying to have them "accidentally" discovered and acknowledged. Jesus had a word for boasting. He said that we should not do our good deeds to be admired. Receive the applause of men if you will. But don't kid yourself—receiving their applause is done at the expense of receiving God's applause[34]. If we were to imagine that we achieved right standing without the aid of grace, then our achievements become our boast. Sadly, that's all it takes to cancel blessings. Only works done without fanfare can add to our heavenly bank balance!

As in the corporate world, the danger is that people are promoted to the point of their incompetency. In other words, perfectly competent people are promoted until they reach positions for which they have no competence. This may lead to whole departments, and sometimes even whole corporations malfunctioning. What follows are all kinds of stresses and strains—everybody bears the brunt of the new boss' incompetence.

An itinerant preacher once told me of his frustration with church board members.

"They are leadership misfits," he protested, "Most of them have never had any authority before, and their new found power goes straight to their heads."

As with social climbers who claw their way to the top of the "A list" where the lime light shines brightest, there are church climbers seeking the limelight where there is glory for themselves. How self-satisfying to flash our religious titles and casually slip our achievements into conversations. Jesus had a word for church climbers. He said that if you want to be first, you must take last place and become a servant to all[19].

But those who walk by grace have no need to be reminded of their undeservedness and of their bedraggledness. They are patently aware that they have contributed naught, and therefore have absolutely naught to boast of—their boast is in Christ alone! Grace acknowledges that we achieved nothing and that Jesus achieved everything. Grace takes the focus off our puny religious accomplishments and puts it squarely on Jesus and His glorious accomplishments. When this happens, our lives become all about Jesus' résumé; not ours.

When we turn our attention away from how good we are, and begin to focus on how good He is, then our story becomes the story of what He has done, rather than the story of what we have done.

If He can forgive us so freely, then who are we to demand remorse and shame of ourselves? Grace and mercy is available for all our shortcomings. Only when we become convinced of His complete forgiveness, can we finally come into agreement with Him, and truly forgive ourselves.

There is a secret to our liberation—it is to continuously forgive ourselves to the same degree that God continuously forgives us. Only then do we accept ourselves—blemishes, shortcomings, warts and all!

When the mighty tower of guilt and regret that rules our lives with remorse and shame is finally torn down brick for brick, then new foundations of self-forgiveness and self-acceptance can be constructed on the bedrock of God's unconditional love. This foundation is solid enough to support the construction of a strong tower of healthy self-worth! Our self-worth has a wonderful way of overflowing, spilling both value and worth onto both friend and foe.

It all starts with accepting God's grace for what it really is—free and undeserved!

We love to honour God, but are we really honouring Him when we insist on dishonouring His blood.

"Dishonouring His blood? Never!" We dishonour His blood when we accept that He has forgiven us, yet cannot forgive ourselves. There can be no greater insult to Jesus? He paid very dearly for our forgiveness; the least that we can do in appreciation, is to agree with Him by letting ourselves off the hook.

We are apt to blame ourselves with negative self-talk. When things don't work out as expected, we turn on ourselves, saying that we deserve nothing better, and then proceed to beat ourselves half to death with self-condemnation and regret. It's as though we are speaking on behalf of "the accuser of the brethren". He just stands by and rubs his hands in glee, not needing to intervene. Hell bent on self-destruction, we do his nasty work for him.

The truth is that no matter how much clemency God grants us, unless we are as kind to ourselves as He is to us, we remain in bondage to guilt and shame. But it is not necessary to put ourselves through the wringer. When we grant ourselves permission to be less than perfect, we make room for self-forgiveness. We have all the tools—let's repent, let ourselves off the hook and get on with living triumphantly! It's not up to God; He has done all He can to convince us. It's entirely in our hands to cast off all guilt and shame, and step into a life more loved—a life of abundance and liberty.

Seeing that He paid so dearly with us in mind, we are at liberty to delight ourselves in the luxury of all He achieved for us. Indulge yourself—it is entirely at His expense—the more we take from His gracious hands, the more He is glorified!

PLASTIC FLOWERS AND PORCELAIN FRUIT

John Wayne embodied the image of the quintessential strong, silent cowboy with idealized values. He was a man of few words, but when he spoke, you could take him at his word. He was his own man—never expecting the approval of others, nor impressed with the attention grabbing antics of pretenders. When he walked into a saloon, a respectful hush fell over the gun toting, tobacco spitting, tough talking patrons—not because he demanded respect, but because of the sheer presence of the man.

While religion has us on the hop, motivating us with unrealistic expectations, we do our best to be all things to all people. An impossible task! So we go with the flow and end up doing stuff that we are not cut out to do. And in our efforts to impress, we end up acting out a charade of holiness, pretending to be something we are not. When we are expected to behave in a certain religious way, we do our level best to meet with expectations, but when we discover the task to be beyond us, we resort to faking it. Even though the thought of being a fraud sickens us to the stomach, we fall in with the rest of the crowd and join the masquerade.

Religion presents us with an image, but that's all it is. It's just an image, and each denomination has its own version.

The way a person prays is often a sure clue as to who his pastor is. Nothing wrong with that—usually commendable proof of discipleship. But discipleship is not meant to be cloning. When our particular version of the creed becomes the only version, it is obvious that we have lost the plot and strayed from the truth. When a believer must forgo his or her identity for the sake of fitting in, something is amiss. When people are no longer themselves, but rather what religion expects of them, alarm bells ought to be sounded.

God didn't design us to be robots—our uniqueness was his idea. What is it that makes a flower arrangement special? Isn't it the variety of blossoms and foliage? The striking star shapes of tiger lilies amongst pom-pom ranunculi; the fullness and rich colours of rose blossoms amongst small white specks of "baby's breath"; the flair of "birds of paradise" amongst everyday daisies; brilliant reds amongst mellow mauves; soft maiden hair ferns amongst stiff vertical straps of flax. We are God's bouquet and He loves arranging us in a way that juxtaposes us with one another—our contrasts accentuating one another's uniqueness and beauty. Our differences should not be interpreted as a threat to divine order, but rather the very thing that makes God's bouquet spectacularly glorious!

We are a dull bunch when we, like the seven dwarfs, march robot like while singing "Hi ho! Hi ho! it's off to church we go! Lah lah, Lah lah, Lah lah, Lah lah, Hi ho! Hi ho!" At least the seven dwarfs had the freedom to be different. But where conformity of thought is required, there is no place for individual identities. Nobody seems to see the danger coming, so we fall in with the crowd and do the religious thing. We forget that it is our individuality that makes us attractive to God and to each other.

When we must conform to find acceptance in a group, we have not found love; we have found manipulation. In this environment, we love because we must; not because we do! Sadly, religion can't afford to accept us as we are; there are expectations to be met! But contrived love is fragile love—likely to snap under the weight of the slightest offence. This is not the kind of love God has in mind; His kind does not take offence and never ceases[37].

God does not want everybody to conform to one man's ideas about religion, no matter how sound they may seem. A bunch of identical white daisies do not catch the eye in the way that a skilfully arranged bouquet of wildly contrasting colours and shapes do. Conformity lacks the impact of contrasts in God's majestic floral arrangement of believers.

Lack of variety is easily explained away with such religious sounding concepts as "spiritual fathering" and "shepherding", but even earthly fathers encourage their children to discover their own talents and identities. Wherever sons are required to follow in dad's footsteps in career or business, unless their hearts are in it, unhappiness and failure soon follow.

We are who we are! And each of us have a different flavour to add to the mix. Love comes in many forms, but the moment it is regimented, any semblance of sincerity is lost! Without sincerity, love can hardly be thought of as genuine. To be genuine, it must be spontaneous and unstructured.

Conformity does not only rob the church, it also robs the individual of the wonderful freedom that Jesus died to give. He releases and liberates. To Him, our diversity is attractive—the very thing He loves about us!

Different denominations exist because of differences of opinion. Where on earth did we get this idea from? Certainly not from God! He loves diversity. How can He possibly enjoy seeing His children quarrelling over inflexible opinions? How did our diversity become a reason for animosity? Shouldn't we be enjoying each other's diversity? Shouldn't it be reason for unity—unity in diversity—a concept foreign to religious minds!

Nothing pleases religion more than when everybody within the group holds to the same opinion on dogma. But if everybody within a group thinks the same, then it is clear that none of them have the freedom to think for themselves—clear evidence of religious crafting. When Jesus said that we should be one, He did not have vacant mindlessness in mind; He was referring to oneness in the spirit of love.

Religion's high expectations are surreptitiously imposed, pressurizing innocent followers into looking good. But here is the problem—looking good without being good is what hypocrisy is—

nothing short of a lie, albeit a white one—if there is such a thing. If our Christian charades were criminal offences, whole congregations would be arrested at the church door.

We may be falling apart on the inside, but have opted to play act the part of having it all together. We feel we must preserve our "super spiritual" image and keep our weaknesses secret. Religion forces us to project an appearance of piety, even though we may be all messed up on the inside. What a contemptible bunch of frauds we have become!

"How are you?" they ask.

"Just fine thank you!" we lie.

When we dare to be honest and say, "My world is falling apart", we may get a retort such as, "What kind of a faith confession is that?" It may even lead to an unsolicited lesson on the importance of correct faith confessions. So we conclude that it is better to keep our pain to ourselves and just suffer in silence. We have allowed religion to make plastic flowers and porcelain fruit of us!

We may be able to keep up the pretence of a harmonious marriage in front of our religious friends but fight like cat and dog the moment we reverse the car out of the church parking.

We may be able to deal with a particularly nasty confrontation with a modicum of decorum, but don't push us too far—we have a breaking point—exceed it at your peril! You will very quickly discover the reality of who the mild mannered, polite and gentle saint really is! What is this flaky saintliness all about?

Religion gives us the instructions but cannot give us the enablement to carry out the instructions, so we do the next best thing—we fake it! With self-deception, we can avoid facing up to our short comings. We settle for deception and accept the deception of others. We make as good a life as we can out of churchified play acting—it works—everybody else is into the same flaky game.

Quite frankly, there is nothing quite as contemptible as a self-deceived disciple living the lie of pretence for appearance's sake. There can be no pleasure in competing for points when we're competing with smug superiority and conceited puffed-up-ness. We make ourselves detestable, when our heads are swollen with our own deluded sense of religious importance. Spiritual pride and fake piety are nauseating, to say the least. We may be able to dazzle each other with our spiritual accomplishments, but when will the penny drop? We simply cannot dazzle God!

To the degree that I deny my state of abject poverty, I deny God the right to affect my heart with His unmerited love and favour. Ever opened your heart in love to a trusted friend, only to have it cruelly crushed in betrayal? Imagine how God must feel when we spurn his unmerited love in the supposed interests of "holiness".

Where did we ever get the idea that we cannot have both grace and holiness at the same time? But then again, that's religion for you—it has its own weird ideas. We are forced to choose between "extreme grace" and "holiness". But the truth of the matter is that nobody can make themselves holy! Such a lofty ideal is simply not humanly achievable! Let's face it, we all started out unholy. Any attempt from an unholy person to be holy could only produce more un-holiness! Humanity is only capable of giving the appearance of holiness—a far cry from the real deal!

True holiness can only be produced by a source that is already holy and that's why we require divine grace. Without it, our holy appearances are nothing more than a sham! Most believers embrace grace, but most have set limits to it. But by imposing limits upon grace, our achievements overshadow Jesus' achievements. It's not supposed to be about us; it supposed to be about Jesus.

We cannot blame believers for being suspicious of grace. Nobody is going to entrust their future to something that they have been cautioned to be weary of. Grace has gotten a bad rap from so many pulpits for so long that it is no wonder that it is treated with scepticism. "Stay away from sloppy agape", we hear it said. What an awful thing to say about God's most wonderful gift to humanity! God is never sloppy about anything; least of all in the way He loves us.

Children don't just leap from the branch of a tree in the hope that just anybody will catch them. But with dad it is different. If he says jump, the kid jumps without a moment's hesitation—what's to fear if dad is near?

Where does this kind of trust come from? Love! That's where! Dad would rather hurt himself than allow his little one to get hurt, and the little tyke knows it. This level of trust takes time to blossom. Similarly, if we are able to accept that God really loves us in our present less than perfect condition, and that He will continue to love us, even if we do nothing to improve ourselves, we will find ourselves trusting Him without hesitation!

Confidence engendered by such depth of love brings us to the point where we are prepared to risk everything on one thing and one thing only, and that one thing is God's unconditional love. A leap of faith is required to jump from the tree of religious self-reliance and self-achievement into the loving arms of a gracious Daddy, who could care less about what we've achieved. All that matters to Him is that we are His little boy or girl.

Only a deep awareness of His unmerited love can move us from scepticism to unshakable trust. We acquire this kind of rock solid assurance from knowing Him—to know Him is to know how deeply we are loved! Sermons can help us to know Him on an intellectual level, but it takes more than sermons to know him in an intimate way. When we are in His loving embrace, nothing else counts for a row of beans—we are safe, secure, provided for, healed and favoured! What is there to fear[138]? What could be better? Nothing else comes close!

PROGRAMMES—A POOR SUBSTITUTION

In the book of Acts, where the church's glorious beginnings are recorded, the church started out with real interaction between God and believers. In our day and age it has evolved into something very different. What was once God and people centric is now programme and performance centric. There is a set order of service—a church sandwich if you wish. Imagine a Dagwood sandwich stacked in layers of onion, lettuce, tomatoes, bacon, fried egg and cheese, between two slices of bread. It's made according to a set recipe and it always turns out exactly the same. A Dagwood Church Service is a set order of service which is served between a slice of opening prayer and a slice of closing prayer—entirely predictable.

Imagine visiting your best mate. He ushers you into his home and pulls out a printed agenda. Starting at the top, he works his way through the list. He does all the talking; you obediently listen. The order is exactly the same as on your last visit—entirely predictable. In the face of such measured monotony, what chance would there of enjoying his company? Let's face it, even the thought of such a stiff relationship is ludicrous!

It's the informality of our liaisons, and the warmth of our companionships that glue our relationships together. Rigid schedules, and stone cold protocols lack these vital ingredients. It's the same with Jesus. If He is the best friend we're ever going to have, why would we insist on boring him with such obvious churchified dreariness?

"That doesn't apply to us! We are a lively church!" you may be protesting. In that case, a good question to ask oneself would be, "How much of our liveliness is pre-programmed and expected of us, and how much of it is impromptu, heartfelt and spontaneous?"

The book of Acts has left us with a clear record of the early church. It was run very differently to the formalised modern-day church service. In our day and age, instead of saints gathering in an informal setting of home hospitality with face to face interaction, as in earlier days; we are seated in rows in a theatre, waiting for the show to begin. The only fellowship is with the back of a stranger's head in the next row.

For many, church has come to be the place where they can ease their consciences—discharging their weekly obligation towards God. For others it's a case of, "I dare you to make me laugh and keep me entertained for an hour and a half". We have created enormous religious enterprises, and now we must appease them— their demands are high!

Little opportunity is given to communal sharing of God's word—little time devoted to touching one another with His gracious love—little chance of sharing testimonies and hardships with one another. People seldom have the time of day to lend an ear, much less to bear one another's burdens. In many cases, meetings have become a matter of providing an appreciative audience for a talented speech maker—a platform for clever pulpiteering. It is often difficult to know who is being applauded— God, or the toastmaster? Sadly, in many cases, we have exchanged spiritual visitation for eloquent oratory. If ever there was a poor trade off, it is this!

There is little opportunity to get to know and understand one another's struggles. People are reluctant to admit to acquaintances, never mind strangers, that they are not cutting it. We would rather not risk being seen to be less than religion expects of us. Then there is the matter of sharing resources and helping each other—how can we do it when our resources have been committed to the commendable charities of the church.

Modern day house churches would be closer to the real deal. But it all goes horribly wrong when house church is simply a regurgitation of last Sunday's sermon. All too often it becomes a mini version of Sunday's meeting with somebody else taking centre stage.

A prim and proper highly organised house church leader visited someone else's house church. What he saw there horrified him. They had neither programme nor structure—people just arrived and casually chatted over coffee and cookies. He thought to himself, "What a shambolic excuse for a house church!" Then someone said, "Let's hear what God wants to tell us". A hush fell over the group—the visitor became decidedly uncomfortable with the long drawn out silence—he felt especially awkward for first time visitors, wondering what they were making of this disorganised lot.

Then something truly remarkable happened—without any apparent reason, there was sniffling here and there, and then quiet sobbing from others. God had pitched up and was dealing with individuals in a personal way that no three point sermon could. The Holy Spirit had taken over and was doing a fine job without any help from churchified structures, sermons or programmes.

Whether gatherings are small or large, church is meant to be about community. But when size becomes more important than intimacy, the vitality of Christian fellowship gets lost in the crowd. We ought to stay mindful of the model given to us in the book of Acts, where spontaneity and intimacy had no bounds. Structured services can so easily structure the Holy Spirit's participation out. Often He is relegated to a minor slot in the programme, and little or no time given to communal fellowship. Then when He is actually allowed in, He is subjected to the control of the elders, who vet and amend testimonies, words of knowledge and prophecies before being made public. Obviously, when spontaneity is controlled, it is no longer spontaneous.

So-called "non-traditional" churches often criticise the liturgy of "traditional" churches, whilst their own practices are just a newer version of liturgy. Like clockwork, you always know exactly what's coming next. First a prayer, followed by a solo or quartet, followed by church announcements. Then a time of setting the spiritual tone with praise, followed by worship, climaxing with a sermon, and concluding with a song and a prayer. Charismatic believers who live in glass houses should not throw stones. "Non-traditional" churches are in the self-same rut; only a little showier—glitzy rituals with a touch of pizazz! But entertainment is a poor substitute for the glorious presence of the Holy Spirit.

It's not that there is anything wrong with Christian entertainment, but a problem arises when church programmes become a diversion from the real deal. A church might boast that it has no rituals—that is debatable. A ritual is defined as "a procedure that is followed regularly". Isn't that an accurate description of what happens in most churches whether traditional or not?

We are complex in our makeup and need all the elements of our being to be nourished. We are spirit and therefore need to be spiritually stimulated with the word of God and the Holy Spirit. There is hole within all of us that can only be filled with His love. Love sets the stage for honesty. There is no further need for posturing. Nothing is hidden from Him—our darkest secrets don't scare Him—He understands our every weakness.

We live in a body that needs physical exercise and sustenance, the body's fuel. We have an intellect that needs to be intellectually challenged with problem solving. We are social and need to engage and interact with each other to form bonds of camaraderie and friendship. We are emotional and need love, humour, laughter, sadness and weeping. We have five senses that need to see beauty and squalor; taste the best and the worst cuisine; listen to harmonic and discordant music; smell roses and decay.

When the balance between spiritual and temporal is upset, and any aspect of life becomes crowded out by any other aspect of life, we end up being lesser beings. When our lives are all spiritual and little else, we become single note songs, instead of symphonies— we just don't have enough notes within us to create full chord harmonies. Religion has a way of attending to one aspect, while others spin out of kilter.

The original Church of the book of Acts is as good a model as we have to go by. No mention is made of Christian entertainment or church programmes of any shape or form, because church was not in any way formalised in the way it is today. Believers simply gathered in each other's homes. What followed was Spirit lead. God himself spoke to them through prophecy, words of knowledge, tongues and interpretation. There was opportunity for breaking of bread, prayer, sharing of faith, and just plain and simple social interaction around a meal.

In our day and age, the written word of God plays a central role in our services. This was not the case in the early church—they didn't have the New Testament—it hadn't been compiled yet. The Bible, as we know it, came many centuries later. If you lived in Ephesus, you had one short letter from Paul and a few shared letters from a couple of other apostles that were doing the rounds. That was it!

Not having the written word of God had its advantages—these folk were more attuned to hearing and sensing God directly, and this direct communication with him was every bit as meaningful as the Bible is to us, only a whole lot more personal. What could possibly be more meaningful than one-on-one communion with God?

In our mission to get as much Bible reading done as possible, we follow the "read through the bible in one year plan", ploughing through the pages, crowding out any possibility of hearing the Spirit. In this sense, an innocent commitment becomes a stumbling block to hearing from God. There is no question about it—God does speak to us through His written word, but there is so much more that He wants to tell us. When we listen out for Him in the chores and joys of our everyday lives, we discover how sweet His fellowship really is.

Unfortunately, many centuries ago, the freedom of ordinary believers, living in the grace of hearing God for themselves, was gradually phased out. Church leaders, in their thirst for power and control, took on the role of hearing God for the people, thus robbing them of their blood bought connection with God. Eventually the right to hear God became the exclusive province of the clergy. Instead of resulting in a closer walk with God; it distanced believers from Him. Ultimately, the freedom and liberty that Jesus died to give mankind, became so distant that it finally slipped over the horizon and disappeared from humanity. The clergy, in its wisdom, had usurped the most essential elements of humanity's intimacy with God. The beauty of a grace relationship, characterised by freedom and liberty, evaporated into thin air.

This was supposedly done for our own good. The less freedom we had, the more we could be controlled and monitored—herded into a more righteous way of living. Sadly, control sent the church into a downward spiral until all semblance of spiritual relevance was lost. Humanity had been consigned to the bleakness of the "dark ages". At that time, ordinary believers no longer had the slightest vestige of freedom. Religious control of believers was officially sanctioned and fully vested in the clergy. No one was allowed to own a Bible, allowing the clergy to indoctrinate with impunity—no one dared challenge them! Anyone daring to shed new light on dogma was labelled a heretic and summarily burnt at the stake. Once ordinary believers had been defrauded of their royal priesthood, freedom and grace, it became a simple matter to use fear to manipulate and control.

Many of the great Cathedrals of Europe were built on fear money manipulated from the poor in lieu of penance. Forgiveness of sins could be purchased at a price. Before they knew what had hit them, the gospel of freedom and grace had degenerated into un-gospel, fear and bondage.

The church has come a long way since then with revolutionary reformations and wild fire revivals. Over the centuries, God sent reformers to restore grace to the church, but sadly, with the passage of time, the precious gift of grace relapsed into just another religious ritual. History has shown that, wherever a grace awakening arose, it was very quickly snuffed out by those in charge. By and large, the church extends endless grace to sinners, but fails to extend the same measure of grace to believers.

I asked a church leader to define grace. To my horror he came up with two very different definitions, one for sinners, for which he correctly defined grace to be unlimited, and another completely different definition for believers. To him believers are not granted the same measure of grace because they are required to live holy lives. He couldn't accept that our on-going development in holiness is as much a work of grace as was our initial salvation. If perchance he was right, then we would have to conclude that the grace that saved us is not potent enough to keep us saved—we must give God a hand—He is not as almighty as we have been told.

We ought never to forget that we were granted grace at a time when we were enemies of the cross. Surely if God grants so much grace to His enemies, He will grant more to His friends, and even more to the intimate members of His family, the very ones He perfected with His blood.

Even sinful earthly fathers are more concerned for the wellbeing of their own families than for the wellbeing of their enemies. To imagine that mortals are more caring than God, would be tantamount to saying that mortals are holier than God. Such a notion is unconscionable! But there are control freaks who feel duty bound to keep us striving to reach the mark. Let's face it, no-one has ever reached the mark, and no-one is ever likely to reach it. It is something that is only obtainable without merit through grace!

In our personal venture of striving for the mark, we achieve little. If we dare to attempt it without the empowerment of God's grace, we will find something other than sanctification. Mankind simply cannot sanctify itself; it takes the grace of God to do that. But thankfully, with the help of grace, holiness is a breeze!

It is easy for our enemy to keep us entrapped in self-effort. Striving for holiness sounds so religious, yet our most earnest endeavours remain a gazillion miles short of what holiness is! Let's face it, according to Isaiah, we are only capable of producing filthy rags[135]!

Satan knows that our utmost is not enough to achieve holiness. He also knows that, for as long as we are chasing our tails for holiness, we will overlook the true source of holiness—it is in grace and grace alone—holiness does not even exist outside of grace! Our flawed attempts at holiness will keep us away from the sanctifying ways of the Spirit of grace. Sadly, the religious notion that we are able to make ourselves holy is often given more credence than the sanctifying work of the "Spirit of grace". Do we seriously believe that our holy making can outdo God's holy making? Well of course not! Our finest efforts fall horribly short of His holy standard! Disillusionment is the only reward for anyone brave enough to tackle the task of holy making without the help of grace.

Let's face it—the Spirit is infinitely more able than self-effort. The value that we receive from being unconditionally loved gives us permission to love ourselves. The urge to find this value in sin fades.

Religion sees grace as a door to permissive sin, when in reality it is a door to overcoming sin—something that religion simply cannot do. The beauty of grace is that it sanctifies our actions without our help. It is easy to trust one who loves us so immensely—easy to submit to Him.

The Church is meant to be the place where grace liberates, but is more often than not the place where legalism restricts and confines. Ecclesiastical judicial dictates are given more weight than our blood bought liberty. Christ's most magnificent gift of grace to mankind is simply side-lined for the sake of "God ordained" church governance. Sadly, many well-meaning guardians of religion have convinced followers to be suspicious of freedom. Grace often gets a bad rap, but let's face it, without grace, what are we left with? Nothing more than Buddhism, Hinduism or Mahammadism—to put it plainly, we have absolutely nothing at all!

Caring clergymen are often convinced that the freedom of grace would be dangerous in the hands of ordinary mortals. They may think, "They're not mature enough to handle such freedom." To their way of thinking, given the freedom, believers are likely to make decisions detrimental to their spiritual wellbeing. Consequently, they construct moral fences, and take personal responsibility for the holiness of their flocks. Believers are told what to do and what not to do—what to think and what not to think. People who are programmed in this way tend to lose their individuality, and therewith, their God ordained creativity.

We saw freedom and creativity in God's prototypes—firstly Adam before his fall, and then Jesus. Freedom to be ourselves in personality and creativity is the idea of a brilliant mind—the mind of an imaginative Creator. But grace, freedom and liberty simply cannot survive mass managed religious conformity.

Once our freedom has been forfeited, we drift aimlessly, ever closer towards our own "dark ages". Grace, freedom and liberty are at the very core of our faith—remove them and all we are left with is a devotion to religious monotony. Without grace, the gospel is nothing more than empty meaninglessness. "Dear Lord, spare us from slavery to pastoral autocracy. Shield us from the deathly clutches of mystical formulas."

Freedom is at the very core of Christianity—without it, Christianity collapses into a heap of forms and formulas. To be frank—without the freedom of grace, Christianity does not even exist!

What was the Bible referring to when it said that they have a form of godliness but deny the power thereof[38]? It was referring to denying the power God embodied in grace; substituting it with religious striving. This scripture is unfolding before our very eyes in much of today's religiosity. Whether "traditional" church or "contemporary", the danger is precisely the same!

GOD EXPECTS LESS FROM US

While Religion is expecting holiness from us; God is more realistic. He knows that sanctifying our actions is not an event but a process—never complete this side of eternity. And He is perfectly comfortable with that.

In the first place, how can we know what holiness is when each denomination draws the holiness line in a different place? And more than that, the goal posts keep moving. What was once unacceptable is now perfectly acceptable. Let's be reasonable—they can't all be right! All that we can deduce from all this confusion is that none of them are right!

Where does God draw the line? According to the Bible, He doesn't have a line. Jesus only gave us definite instructions on a handful of issues. Then He gave us a broad framework of principles to cover the rest, summarising them in one sentence saying, "Do unto others what you would have them do unto you". We call it the golden rule[48]. This rule requires that we give the same degree of consideration, respect and love to others that we would wish to have for ourselves. Isn't it amazing how Jesus boils everything down to one thing and one thing only—nothing other than grace?

It is not enough to be satisfied with receiving this priceless commodity; it remains incomplete until it is given away to people who are as undeserving as ourselves. To fail to do so would make us guilty of "selective selfishness"—a social ill that should not be incubated in the halls of religion.

Jesus left us with two commandments. He said that we must love the Lord with every ounce of our being, and then love our neighbour as much as we love ourselves[95].

On our own, we are ill-equipped for the task—we simply cannot measure up to God's standard. If we fail often enough in our right making attempts, we end up with a defeatist's attitude. With damaged self-esteem we cease to expect God's best, and take life's knocks lying down, thinking that we have no right to expect anything better.

According to Jesus, there is a limit to our love. We can only love others to the degree that we love ourselves. If we loath ourselves, we end up loathing everybody else. Unless we can accept that God loves us unconditionally, we will not find it easy to love ourselves unconditionally. If we don't truly love ourselves, we're unlikely to truly love anybody else. Is there any wonder that there is so much loathing going around?

What is the cure for this self-despising disease? It is to discover that we are loved exactly as we are right now without any pressure upon us to change. If we can understand that the pressure to change ourselves is off, we can relax and be real. If grace is allowed to run its life modifying course, the need to strive for it comes to an end. If God can love us unconditionally, why can't we? His love gives us permission to love ourselves in a healthy way. Divine love is like a hypodermic booster shot of self-worth! Healthy self-love empowers us to love God and others more completely. It all begins with discovering that God loves us in our present less than perfect state, and that He will continue to love us even if we never change.

If we are to love our neighbour, then as with the disciples, we need to know who our neighbour is. Jesus answered this question by telling the story of the good Samaritan[39.] In that story a man went out of his way to help his sworn enemy. Jesus could not have made it any clearer—our love is not to be reserved for the people we like. The genuine God kind of love has no prejudices—it is not limited to the nice to be around folk; the kind hearted and generous folk; the do you no harm dear hearts and gentle people. It breaks through our sensibilities and prejudices and empowers us to love the kind of people that any reasonable person would find repulsive.

Our prisons are bulging with criminals, the dregs of society, and each and every one of them is our neighbour. Seriously? If ever there is a hard pill to swallow, this is it! In Jesus' estimation, we are to consider our worst enemies neighbours. Loving them is something that is not within the ability of humanity, but well within the ability of those rare human beings who have had their hearts transformed by an awareness of the unconditionality of God's love for them.

We are simply not able to manufacture God's kind of love and acceptance. Especially when we are confronted with angry, revengeful, malicious, spiteful, out to get us individuals. When we recognise how immensely we are loved, despite our personal flaws and hang-ups, we in turn find enough love to make room in our hearts for repulsive humanity.

When dealing with controlling and abusive husbands, Paul doesn't bash them over the head with the book of the law. No! He uses a higher motivation. He says that husbands should love their wives as much as Jesus loves His wife, the church[40]. Jesus loves her so much that He laid His life down for her[41]. There's that "love" word again!

When the guardians of religion brought a woman caught in adultery to Jesus, they tested Him to see if He would break Moses' law[42]. The law required that she be stoned to death. Jesus at first ignored their accusations and scribbled in the sand. Then looking up, He said that the one without any sin should cast the first stone. Pretty reasonable, wouldn't you say? The accusers knew their sin, and so guiltily slunk off one by one, until there were none left to accuse her. Jesus asked, "Woman, where are those accusers of yours? Has no one condemned you?" She said, "No one, Lord." And Jesus said to her, "Neither do I condemn you; go and sin no more"[42].

For the religious mind, this is outrageous. Imagine what the sanctimonious of our day and age would say if they came across such "easy grace" and "sloppy agape".

"What were you thinking Jesus? Don't you know that she must confess her sins before she can receive mercy? Why no sinner's prayer Jesus? What about getting her to renounce her sins? She didn't even give the faintest hint that she was sorry. Seriously Jesus! This is a slut from the wrong side of the tracks".

Doesn't He realise that such loose religion could result in her walking straight back into the arms of her paying customers? She got absolution without even asking for it. Jesus sure did botch this one, didn't He?

Or on the other hand, if Jesus handled it correctly, why is His way so at odds with the religious way? The answer is simple. If ever anybody was anti-religion, it was Jesus! Jesus is not the founder of the Christian religion; He is the founder of the anti-religious movement—better described as "the grace revolution"[43]. This revolution runs counter to religion, granting salvation where it is not deserved—going so far as to love saints, even when they bungle their precious testimonies.

Jesus led a thieving criminal to paradise while hanging on the cross[44]. He didn't ask him to confess his sins or to repeat the sinner's prayer, yet He granted him a place in paradise. By the way, the sinners prayer does not appear anywhere in the Bible. The only prayer that the thief prayed was, "Jesus, remember me when you come into your kingdom", nothing more! He didn't even have the religious etiquette to end his prayer with an "amen". He made no mention to Jesus of his many sins—not even a word of apology or remorse, not even a word of repentance.

There is only one word for Jesus' extravagant love for us—it is "outrageous!" How do we get our minds around something that is as magnanimous as His grace? To our religiously slanted thinking, His generosity borders on irrationality! Think about it—surely Jesus should have expressed some measure of disgust, or at least have made it clear to the thief that He disapproved of his behaviour. How could He be so soft on sin? Shouldn't He have been more blunt and to the point? After all, this was no ordinary criminal—ordinary criminals were jailed; not crucified.

The Bible is quite clear on this point. It says that whoever calls on the name of the Lord shall be saved[45]. This scripture does not have an addendum that says, "In addition, he must always be up to date with confession, promise to live the rest of his life for God, or promise to do his best to not sin." There is nothing of the kind!

"Ah!" you may be protesting, "You cannot take one scripture without cross referencing it with other scriptures on the same subject. The collective meaning of all these scriptures must be taken as a whole before coming to such a decisive conclusion".

Really? Well that certainly was not the case on this particular day in history. These were Peter's words—he was addressing people who did not have a single scripture at hand to cross reference. Three thousand of them received salvation based on this instruction alone.

Did they repent? Certainly! Peter went on to instruct them to do so! But, repentance has come to mean something quite different in this day and age to what it meant then. Self-condemnation is not repentance—repentance is not about being all cut up and miserable, and beating oneself half to death with remorse. It is not even making promises never to repeat our sins. Yes sorrow goes together with repentance, but it has nothing in the world to do with dragging ourselves into a dark cloud of self-despisement. Repentance does not bring us into remorse and shame. No! No! No! Repentance brings us out of remorse and shame!

Religion has added its own convenient twist to redefine words— now we all misunderstand them. Of course, nobody would blame us for being remorseful and sorry, but that is not what is meant by repentance. Repentance means to reconsider something and think differently about it. A matter of forsaking our flawed way of thinking to adopt the Kingdom's flawless way of thinking.

With grace, there is no need to force ourselves; rather we find ourselves behaving differently and have no explanation for it! It wasn't we who forsook our old self-destructive, self-absorbed, narcissistic lifestyles; they forsook us! Not by grit and determination; by transformation! Repentance is mind transformation and transformed individuals behave differently! How are we transformed? Certainly not by the renewing of our actions. It is by renewing our minds! It's what repentance is! It starts with a revolution of the mind. It's a fact of life: Transformed minds transform actions! We are no longer trying to be righteous; we are already the righteousness of God in Christ[77] and this mind-set plays out in our daily living!

The Bible tells us that we are what we think[113]. Our wrong thinking gets us into all sorts of trouble, and our right thinking propels us into favour and privilege. Religious thinking has a way of making us conscious of our sins, causing us to feel unworthy of God's glory. Wherever religion reigns, wavering faith and uncertainty reign. There is always this nagging question for which no-one seems to have an answer, "Have I done enough for God?" But this is decidedly the wrong question!

"Oh, how I wish I had done this or that", are the regretful words of people living in the darkness of their pasts. Religion often focuses on our failures, and the guilt of it holds us imprisoned in our pasts; whereas grace overlooks our failures, reminds us of our righteousness in Christ, raising our hopes, giving us good reason to expect more. Hope is not rear view mirror vision, it is forward vision. Hope propels us into a brighter future!

With grace, our sin is no longer the issue; the glory of God within us is the issue[123/67]! Just think of it! We have the glorious privilege of carrying God's glory! Seriously? The thought of it is enough to make one giddy! What is this glory? It is a dowsing of His goodness. Before we know it, the supernatural has become second nature—the miraculous, the new norm!

Jesus so desperately wanted our friendship, but as a holy God, He simply could not afford to have His holiness compromised with our sins. As much as He requires holiness, try as we may, we are simply incapable of attaining His holy standard—it's far too high for mere mortals! It is obvious—nobody gets it right. So if He considered us worth the trouble, He would have to step in and do it for us. To do it, He would have to make sin a non-issue, but for that to happen, sinless human blood would have to be shed. We all know that no such blood runs in the veins of humanity. The only way was for God to become a man, take mankind's sin upon Himself, and shed His very own sinless blood to redeem mankind. When we come to realise the depths of love that caused a holy God to allow His Son to be contaminated and disgraced with the filth of our sin, then yielding to His Spirit ceases to be a "have to" and soon becomes a "want to". When we are yielded, sanctification has carte blanche to run its life altering course in our lives.

As citizens of the kingdom, we have entered the realm of the miraculous. But while we are of the opinion that our good standing with God is in question, the miraculous remains no more than a pipe dream. Although we have become the walking, talking expression of God in all His glory[67], our wrong thinking keeps us out of the miraculous. We contain everything that God is—the entire Godhead dwells within us bodily. But what is the value of it if we are allowing our shortcomings to define us and disqualify us from moving in the glory. God has defined us as entirely righteous[77], and given us His glory[67]. We are fully qualified to step out in faith!

I cannot stress this enough—we should never lose sight of our right standing with our Father—it is shatterproof! The reason that it is rock-solid is because we played absolutely no part in establishing it—it is forever unsoiled by our many sins[123]. We should not be asking whether or not we are in right standing with God; we should be asking whether or not Jesus is in right standing with Him. If He is, so are we[127]. To live with this awareness is to live conscious of the glory of God residing within us.

It makes a world of difference to our confidence when we approach God without the faintest trace of condemnation. A sense of condemnation serves only to foul up faith[124]. While we are unsure of our right standing, we are simply not able to exercise any degree of certainty in prayer. Instead of our requests bursting with confidence, we end up with pitiful pleading, more akin to begging, than to standing in unshakable confidence—an essential ingredient of faith.

When we are hesitant—unsure of our right standing with God, we tend to avoid His presence, making intimacy with Him most unlikely. Somehow His holiness poses a threat to our comfort zones. His presence comes to mean condemnation, when it should mean liberation from condemnation! Sadly, this makes us sin focused, when we ought to be glory focused. And that's all it takes to draw us into even more sin[21]. Unwittingly, religion, in its sincere attempt to keep sin out of our lives, has succeeded in achieving the reverse. Is there any answer to this sorry predicament? There sure is! While religion is trying to convince us to do something about our sorry state; grace is trying to convince us to draw righteousness from the righteousness imputed to us by Jesus. It is called walking by the Spirit. And while we are doing so, we are not fulfilling the lusts of the flesh[131].

Being the recipient of unmerited love and favour and being counted righteous for no good reason of our own making, is heart captivating stuff! While we are motivated by love, we can do no harm—no rules needed to help us distinguish right from wrong. Right decision making becomes a product of God's love. He has chosen to channel His love through us to those around us! When we are restrained by love, legalism and religious restraints have nothing further to contribute!

Religion's way to holiness is enormously burdensome. Religion makes up its own set of rules and expects us to conform to them. We do our best, but without grace, our utmost strivings lack the necessary power to oblige. On the other hand, grace assures us that we are held safely in right standing with God. Besides, fighting sin does not help us sin less—fighting sin serves only to stoke sin. Now grace is a very different kettle of fish—rather than making temptations stronger, it makes our resistance to temptations stronger!

Sin springs forth from hearts that are more conscious of their sin than of the glory within them. While our religion has us fighting sins, we do our best. But our best is no better than filthy rags—a kind of self-righteousness offensive to God. Self-righteousness, being self-made, is simply not righteous enough to satisfy a holy God. That being the case, what is the solution? Forsaking sin consciousness for glory consciousness! We find His glory wrapped in grace!

Don't be deceived—godly living is simply not possible without the help of grace! It takes a revelation of His love to adjust our innate thinking. Repentance towards God is not a once-off discharge of religious duty; it is a lifelong collaboration with the Holy Spirit in a continuous process of character shaping.

We are simply incapable of sanctifying ourselves. Sanctification is God's doing and His doing alone—it is not called the fruit of the "Spirit" for nothing. The Spirit's fruit is His doing; not ours! Our finest efforts: our best endeavours to live right, can at best only succeed in producing works of the flesh.

It is interesting to note that the church's strongest criticism of the grace awakening is the belief that God cannot look upon sin. That is certainly so, but that is why He doesn't see our sin; He sees the blood of Jesus[82]! He has chosen not to keep a single record of our sins, no matter how deplorable[132].

Manufactured holiness is not in the least bit holy. Holiness is a product of God's grace and His grace alone! Flesh is only capable of shamming holiness! And faking the fruit of the Spirit makes a farce of Christianity—hypocrisy of the highest order! Sadly, if the Spirit is not producing His fruit, we are left to try and appear to be holy, but looking holy is not the Gospel of our Lord and Saviour!

Our repentances don't obligate God to bless us—they don't earn credits that can be haggled for favours. It doesn't work that way—in fact the reverse is true—repentance is our response to the favour that He has already lavished upon us[15].

It is so easy to fall into the trap of imagining that God's level of favour towards us depends on how current and up to date we are with repentance. But this kind of thinking keeps us out of grace. Our repentances are good, proper and decent, but they do not reinstate our salvation. If we believe that our salvation rests on the state of our practical holiness, then we can never be sure where we stand with Him. We would be bouncing in and out of salvation like a rubber ball attached with elastic to a table tennis bat. One minute saved, and the next, unsaved. Even small issues like bickering and impatience would undo our salvation. Then the onus would lie with us to reinstate our salvation with an appropriate measure of repentance. This would leave us unsaved until we eventually get around to repenting. But this cannot be right—Jesus did not give us a ding-dong salvation!

We must ask ourselves, "Is the blood of Jesus enough, or is it deficient? Does it need our filthy rags to hold it together?" Paul said that this kind of thinking frustrates grace—equivalent to saying that Jesus died in vain[121]. But we are not favoured by reason of our righteousness; we are favoured by reason of the righteousness accredited to us by Christ[122]. God has chosen to treat us as though we have never committed a single sin[82].

This is difficult for religious folk to comprehend, much less to accept. To them grace is too easy to be religious. But that's just it! It is not meant to be difficult, nor is it meant to be religious! Jesus said that His yoke is easy and His burden is light[136]. Contrary to their reasoning, grace does not make us slack in doing good works; it is precisely opposite—grace both empowers and motivates us to do good works.

When Jesus washed the disciples' feet, He said that servanthood is the pathway to blessings[129]. Do we really understand the kind of grace that it took for the Son of God to stoop to washing the smelly feet of filthy fishermen and crooks? Do we really think that we should be any less gracious than Jesus? Let's face it, we cannot serve others with the bad news of religion; we can only serve them with the good news of His grace!

Repentance is not only an essential step towards salvation; it is an on-going grace discipline. But it is not something that keeps us saved. It is the blood of Jesus that keeps us saved. Fortunately, our salvation is not flimsy! Let's be honest, there is always a delay between the time we sin and the time we eventually get around to repenting. If we were to die during such unrepented periods, we would be vulnerable—exposed to the risk of being relegated to an eternity in hell. According to Jesus, even our thought life can make us law breakers. Well, the good news is that God no longer counts our sin against us, period[132]!

There is an awful dilemma facing those who insist that unrepented sin cancels salvation. Their salvation is flawed—they have not found security in Jesus! How can they ever be certain that they will manage to be current and up to date enough with repentance on the day that death takes them by surprise? Quite obviously, this notion cannot be right—unrepented sin cannot cancel something as secure as God's unequivocal declaration of our right standing with Him. He no longer remembers our sins[101]! End of story!

Does this information make you want to go out and indulge your senses in sin? Anybody who would take grace to be an invitation to sin has not understood the purpose of grace. Grace was not given to empower us to sin; grace was given to empower us to overcome sin!

Yes there are requirements to receiving God's favour—no, we cannot meet the requirements. The whole reason that the gospel is "good news" is that everything required of us has already been fully met by Jesus—nothing further is expected of us, except that we love and believe.

Yes, we can walk outside of His grace—all it takes is to seek righteousness by our own merits. Those who have chosen religion over grace have chosen to walk a difficult road. God's word reveals how to tap into His grace. But for those who live loved, there is nothing arduous about His directions—loved people are delighted to comply with His directions. But the same cannot be said for those who have made grace out to be conditional. They will insist that we have to live right before we can expect to be favoured. The question is, "Are we able to live right enough?" Good question! The short answer to this crucial question is a resounding "NO!" But take heart, the good news is that although we cannot achieve right living by striving for it, grace has achieved it for us. It all goes around what we understand of His goodness and grace.

Salvation transforms the core spiritual component of man, while repentance transforms our soulish component (our minds). Salvation is a spiritual transformation. Repentance is a thinking transformation. It is not a promise to live without sinning. As mortals, it is beyond our ability to keep such a lofty promise. On the other hand, as mortals, we can turn to grace and find mercy for our past, present and future waywardness. Although we do not possess the power to stop sinning, the discovery of God's undying love for us, despite our sinfulness, has an immense influence upon the way we live.

What is the story of grace? It's the story of unfaithful people through whom the faithfulness of God's unconditional love flows. Why doesn't He choose more suitable vessels? Good question! Why choose unfaithful people? Well, frankly, He doesn't have that luxury. There are no such candidates to choose from. He has no option but to choose from the raggedy bunch that we are!

Grace is God's unique language of love. He says, "I adore you; watching over you with the delight of a lover; I cherish your every word, and although I expect you to fall short more often than you think you will, I have already provided enough grace to deal with all of your blunders".

What we do with the grace of God is the litmus test of our relationship with Him. Do we use her to get saved and then push her out into the cold, or do we suckle at her breasts, stopping only to take short breaths—intoxicated with thoughts of being cherished. Here's the crucial question: Are we driven by what's expected of us, or are we so high on His love, that what's expected of us doesn't need a mentioned? What's expected of us by religion is so often not what's important, but rather what makes us look good. Religion requires holiness; grace motivates holiness—it accomplishes so much more than the unachievable saintly picture painted by religion.

In Ken Blanchard's best seller, "The One Minute Manager", he explains that to effectively motivate people, you must catch them out when they are doing something well, rather than when they are doing something wrong. By turning a blind eye on people's blunders and mistakes, and only acknowledging their good efforts and praiseworthy achievements, a self-worth is engendered in a person that results in better performance and deeper company loyalty. While this is not a perfect metaphor for grace, it does illustrate that even shallow love possesses the power to draw the very best out of people.

When grace turns a blind eye to our faults, and loves us regardless of them, we begin to operate on the clean fuel of "want to" rather than on the dirty fuel of "must do". Before we know it, His will has become our will!

When we are intoxicated with God's love for us, we find ourselves loving others without trying!

Like the protective antibodies in mothers' milk that give babies additional immunity from infections; love encapsulated in grace, has all the antibodies necessary to fend off the dreaded diseases of self-condemnation and shame. We are who we are, and accepting that we are a raggedy lot in deep need of God's grace, is far more commendable than pretending that we are a tower of strength!

STANDING ON CEREMONY

Religion has taught us to approach God with awe and trembling—and then we wonder why He is always so distant. This religious distortion had not been taught to the disciples. At first, they didn't even understand that Jesus was God in the flesh. Sure they recognised that He was the Messiah, but they had no idea that the Messiah would be any different to Moses. It was only very much later that Peter first perceived that Jesus was actually God in the flesh.

They related to Him as a friend, not as a god. The fact that they saw Him as a good teacher, didn't in any way change the informality of their liaisons. Imagine how lovely it must have been for Jesus to have people relating to Him in a natural and informal way. Like you and me, I can only imagine that He appreciates honesty, even if it comes with behaviour that is decidedly less than perfect.

Jesus didn't make a fuss about His deity; in fact, although He was the Son of God, He chose to be known as the son of man. Only on rare occasions, when He was pressed for an answer, did He acknowledged that He is the Son of God.

Consider the way we worship—do we do it in the form of flattery? Empty religious flattery towards God cannot possibly impress the omniscient One who knows manipulation when he sees it coming—nothing about us is hidden from Him. I can only imagine that He would be just as unmoved by the hollowness of being buttered up as would we.

One wonders how differently the disciples would have treated Jesus if they had really known who He was. Imagine Peter inviting Jesus to go fishing. Instead of, "Hey Jesus! Want to go fishing?" it would be, "Oh, Thou great and mighty Jehovah, creator of the heavens and of the earth and all that is in them. Hear the cry of the hearts of Thine humble servants. Wilt Thou cometh fishing with these Thine lowly wayfarers who art ever in Thine most divine and holy service?"

Imagine Jesus having to put up with such wordy nonsense. Would He have been impressed? I don't think so! Such stiff ceremony and false formality would have destroyed any possibility of intimacy in a heartbeat.

While Jesus walked the earth, He introduced us to an intimate way of fellowshipping with God. Protocol was abolished to make way for a warm welcome and close friendship.

We may ask the Father for anything in Jesus' name—Jesus promised that the Father will do it[103]. And believe me—if we can take anybody at their word, it would be our heavenly Papa. Now we have ready access to our Father—something He always wanted. It was how He fellowshipped with Adam and Eve on His visits to the garden in the cool of the day. They had no reason to feel insecure in His presence, and found it easy to be open and honest with Him. The disciples rediscovered the simplicity of Adam's intimacy. No need to stand on ceremony—no need for airs and graces.

It wasn't too long after Jesus had shown us how He prefers to be engaged in fellowship, that religion invented an officious way of approaching Him. Intimate companionship was not respectful enough for religious folk. But let's face it, in formalising our personal relationships, religion has defrauded us! How can we be intimate with our ever loving Papa while standing on ceremony? Religious protocol has no room for the casual ease that was so typical and normal for the disciples. Imagine how off-putting it must be for a person, who knows us intimately, to put up with the religious formalities of feigned respect.

After He had shown us how open and genuine we could be with Him, we found a way of distancing ourselves from Him in a litany of ritualistic mumbo jumbo. Although meant to resemble what were once genuine interactions with God, rituals are poor counterfeits with watered down spiritual significance. Why on earth would we settle for counterfeits after been awarded the original?

A copy of a piece of art work is never as valuable as the original. Religion is no more than a poor attempt at forgery. We have a blank canvas in front of us, we can choose to copy religion's paint by numbers, or we can paint from our hearts. Like parents who appreciate their first grader's innocent attempts at painting a portrait of mom and dad, so God appreciates our feeble, yet genuine communion with Him. He is not expecting anything more than a first grader's childish attempts. He takes whatever creativity we bring, and no matter how childish, He proudly displays it on His fridge door.

Isn't it strange to hear a believer who communicates perfectly well in contemporary everyday English, suddenly switching to archaic highbrow Elizabethan English when he prays—as though Jesus speaks Elizabethan English. When He walked the Planet, He spoke Aramaic and Hebrew—Elizabethan English hadn't even been invented. Who are we kidding when we use grandiose sounding words reserved for public prayers? When we pronounce and annunciate our prayers in a special highbrow tone of voice, are we really impressing God, or could it be that we are hoping to be admired by those who hear our prayers? Neither of these motives can possibly touch the heart of God in the special way that ill-chosen fumbling words of heartfelt love and admiration can. In our attempts at conjuring up a sense of awe in those who hear us, we may gain their admiration, but what is the value of their opinion of us, if all it does is put distance into divine romance?

Jesus received the informal familiarity of his friends without objecting to it—like you and me, He appreciated being on first name terms with His mates.

We sing that wonderful song of intimate friendship, "What a friend we have in Jesus", but when it comes to speaking to our Friend, all intimacy goes straight out the window as we formalise a one sided monologue with a distant Deity.

As a young believer, I always felt intimidated by those in the church who prayed eloquently and formally. Some even added a well-rehearsed tremor to their voices, while others would pitch their voices a few tones deeper in an obvious attempt to sound more reverent and worshipful. The fact that I was not able to compete with such weighty sounding prayers, caused me to avoid public praying at all costs. By comparison, my prayers sounded weak, thin and ordinary—I didn't want to risk sounding less holy, so I never volunteered.

Whenever this subject is broached, there will be those who will say with caution, "It's okay to be informal, as long as we do not become familiar with God". But as a father, God wants a father and child relationship with His beloveds. Unfortunately such a relationship is simply not possible when we approach Him formally and address Him officially.

I watched my daughter with her toddler. While she was doing her best to bottle feed him, he was only interested in playing with her lips, trying to get her to make motorbike sounds. How familiar! But then again, a mother and child relationship thrives on familiarity. God wants us to be children who are comfortable and at home with Daddy. Anything more formal than a parent/child relationship with Papa, would be too stiff to be family.

Familiarity with God does not diminish His divinity; rather it defines His fatherhood more clearly. Reverence is not destroyed by familiarity—we remain patently aware of who the Father is and who the children are. This is not a trite relationship marked with flippancy, but an intimate bond that is as normal as any family relationship could possibly be.

For some reason, many see God the Father as unapproachable, strict and foreboding. But Jesus is not a good Son covering for an angry Dad. Jesus said that if you have seen the Son, you have seen the Father[125]. Whatever you love about Jesus is something that you will find lovable about the Father. If Jesus wants to wash our feet, then you can be sure that it is because our heavenly Father wants to wash our feet.

If you think that this matter is piffling and immaterial, and that we should be talking about deeper truths; well the fact of the matter is that there are no deeper truths than God's love, and nothing more important than receiving it and expressing it back to Him.

Jeremiah said that we should call on God, and that He would show us great and mighty things[81]. Peter said that if we call on the name of the Lord we would be saved[45]. A good prayer could be as short as one simple word like, "Help!"

I must warn you, religion has a stronger pull than grace. Once you have begun to discover the extent of God's love, the tug-o-war begins. You will rejoice in the simplicity and restfulness that comes from being unconditionally loved, and later be persuaded that it cannot possibly be so easy. It is not about qualifying for love; it's about accepting that you are dearly loved—your loving heavenly Father is more desirous to give it to you than you are to receiving it.

Don't expect your friends to move towards grace just because you have—they must discover it for themselves and do so at their own pace. Allow them enough room to stay in religion for as long as it takes. Afford them as much grace as you have been afforded. They may have to witness your grace towards them, before they make any moves towards God's grace. You have the perfect opportunity to display grace by accepting them exactly as they are, without expecting them to agree with you on anything. Abandoning something that is as well structured as religion, especially if it has been a strong anchor in their lives, takes immense courage. The plunge off the high diving board of religion into the depths of grace, with nothing but God's gracious assurance to keep us afloat, can seem daunting at first, but once we step off the board, we are safe in His hands!

PRETEND—JESUS IS WATCHING!

You have heard about the required order for coming into God's presence. Psalm 100 verse 4 tells us to enter through the Temple gates with thanksgiving and to go into the Temple courts with praise. Entering into His presence joyously is wonderful, but the moment it becomes just another required formula, it is no longer wonderful. That's when it transforms from something beautiful into nothing more than empty ritual.

We have been invited to come to the throne of grace to obtain mercy in time of trouble. Rather than just a place to visit occasionally when in trouble, it's a good place in which to take up permanent residence.

Dads love to have their children around and our heavenly Dad is no different. At Dad's place the children have the run of the house. There is no need to ask if it's okay to take anything out of the fridge or pantry—whatever belongs to Dad, belongs to His kids—we are joint-heirs with Jesus[117].

When children are visiting friends, they are expected to be on their best behaviour, but not so at home. Home with Dad is the one place where we can put our guard down and be ourselves. Well behaved or not, God is gracious enough not to notice—it's not called the throne room of "grace" for nothing.

If God were to judge us in the throne room of grace, it would no longer be the throne of grace. Judgement has no place in grace—it is entirely opposite! If God were to invite us to a place of grace and then judge us in that place, we could say that He had gotten us there under false pretences. If there is one certainty in life, it is that our God is holy. It is this that assures us of His integrity—He simply cannot stoop to deception. The moment we enter a place of grace, accusations cease.

While Psalm 100's way of entering into God's presence should not be adopted as just another religious formula, nobody can deny that an upbeat and joyous disposition is a better way to approach a person than with doom and gloom.

What a joy to be in the company of happy and upbeat folk, and by the same token, what a drain to be in the company of negative folk? A defeated disposition is tiresome, draining, and regretfully, deathly contagious; while an enthusiastic disposition is refreshing, uplifting and thankfully, also contagious. Fortunately, we don't have to pretend to be enthusiastic when we're with Dad; just knowing how loved and accepted we are, is a joy in itself!

The Jonty Rhodes legend begun with his diving run-out of Inzamam-ul-Haq during the 1992 World Cup. He will go down in the annuls of cricketing history for the role he played in changing the way the game is played. His agile dives for the ball and pinpoint accurate throws, while still in an off balance position, changed the nature of the game. His style of fielding transformed a leisurely gentleman's pastime into a contest of skill and athleticism.

Besides Jonty's physical contribution, He brought something else of great value to the team. His lively enthusiasm was contagious. No matter whether the team was winning or losing, when he walked onto the field with bat in hand, he wasn't looking down at his feet; he was swinging his bat wildly. His enthusiasm was obvious, and it showed by the volume of the crowd's whooping and applause.

When fielding, you could hear him egging his team mates on—his encouragement pulled the team out of many a deep hole. Ever upbeat, his enthusiasm soon rubbed off on the rest of the team. And enthusiasm proved to be an essential ingredient towards the team's winning mentality.

Enthusiasm comes with eagerness—inspiring and motivating! Without it, a task is nothing more than a chore, but with it, a chore is transformed into a delightsome adventure! The joy of doing something is not found in the task itself, but rather in how gratifying we perceive the task to be. Enjoyment is a matter of choice. Life is a short ride; there are enough dull moments to ruin the journey, but with a measure of enthusiasm, dull takes on a shine and puts a sparkle into life!

I have ruined many a long car journey by turning it into nothing more than a desperate dash to a destination, rather than a pleasant scenic drive. It is a thousand kilometre "hell for leather" sprint from the moment I leave Cape Town to the moment I arrive exhausted in East London—nothing matters except arriving. With this kind of singular mission, the journey becomes a tedious ordeal that must be endured, while the magnificent beauty of the renowned scenic Garden Route flashes by unnoticed.

How sad to live an entire life always grudgingly enduring the immediate moment in the hope that the next will be happier. Far better to squeeze every last drop of enjoyment out of every waking moment, no matter whether good or bad. Whether the road is rough or smooth, there is a way to enjoy every last inch of life's journey. It is surprising what a little zest for life can do to transform the mundane into the extraordinary.

There is an old African adage that says, "If you want to walk fast, walk alone; if you want to walk far, walk with someone".

In God's presence we find good reason to enjoy the ride. Being in the presence of a good friend is just so enjoyable. There is something heart-warming and edifying about sharing happy moments with somebody special. It's something that we can't get from long distance correspondence or photographs. Doing things together adds pleasure to dull chores—shared moments are fun moments. When it comes to playing games, it's not the games; it's with whom we play the games; it's our chums that make our games fun! Companionship on our travels has a way of intensifying the enjoyment of the journey. A walk with a friend turns a mundane stroll into an escapade. When shared with a friend, the enjoyment of a concert lives on long after the curtain has fallen. Outings with friends are so much better when we connect in meaningful ways. Eating out is not so much about the cuisine as it is about the one with whom we share our table—we are enriched by one another's company. Personality to the power of two, is personality squared. And personality squared can be a whole heap of fun!

We are this way because we are made in God's image. He is a warm personable, relational Being. When Adam and Eve sinned, shame broke mankind's relationship with Him, bringing to an end the pleasure of His presence. But Jesus and the Holy Spirit came to change that sad state of affairs. When Jesus dealt with the sin issue, sin and shame lost their right to separate us from God's deep desire to enjoy our company.

We may be hesitant to bother God with our piffling hassles, not realising that we glorify Him more by taking more grace from Him—afterall, He is more willing to give than we are to receive.

David expressed the delight that he found in God's presence when he said that it is where we find fullness of joy and pleasures forevermore[46]. Give it a thought—can anything be better than that?

If we truly want the delight and pleasure that David experienced in God's presence, then we need to make a practice of sensing His presence. It's not something that happens automatically—it's something we do on purpose. Our five senses are the first to vie for our attention, doing all they can to distract us from sensing God's presence.

During the course of each day, there are so many distractions and demands on our time. Idle gaps are very quickly claimed. We all have our own brand of escapism like TV, radio, computer games, movies, reading, sports, ipads, dining out etc. Our five senses will do anything to keep us distracted. The clatter of it all—our world can be very noisy—a case of sensory overload! Unless we deliberately make space for God in our busy days, the delight of hearing His "love talk" is simply crowded out.

Listening out for God is a grace discipline. It's something that Jesus often did. At times He would just take off in a boat to a far off secluded spot. He fasted and prayed for extended periods in the isolation of the wilderness. He sought quietness, far from the maddening crowd where He could hear His Father more clearly. Paul took off for three lonely years to find seclusion in an Arabian desert. In isolation God was able to transform him with His love.

After being trashed by religion, Brian and Jane were at the lowest ebb of their lives. People they deeply love had put them out and turned their backs on them. To make things worse, they were overseas and extremely lonely. In the early hours of one morning, Brian was sitting in his daughter's lounge next to the Christmas tree. He was quietly pondering these heart-breaking events. He called on the Lord for some kind of explanation. What was this all about? What was it leading to?

Then his mind wandered away from his prayers. It wasn't the colourful Christmas tree decorations that held his attention; it was the perfection of the tiny tender shoot at the very top of the tree. For some inexplicable reason, this little sprig absorbed his attention for what must have been the best part of half an hour. After a time of vacant contemplation, he came back to reality with a start, and randomly flipped his Bible open to nowhere in particular. He was rather sleepy and not quite aware of what he was reading. This is what he read: 'And the Sovereign LORD says: "I will take a tender shoot from the top of a tall cedar, and I will plant it on the top of Israel's highest mountain. It will become a noble cedar, sending forth its branches and producing seed. Birds of every sort will nest in it, finding shelter beneath its branches"'[92].

Only after reading it a second time did he come to the realisation that he had just heard the voice of God. God had used the tender shoot on the top of the Christmas tree, followed by a couple of verses about a tender shoot on the top of another tree to make sure that Brian understood that the message was specifically for him. He knows how to get our attention. He had told Brian that he was the tender shoot at the top of the tree, and that he had been plucked, but not discarded— he had been planted on the top of Israel's highest mountain. Suddenly all the pain made perfectly good sense!

The rough send-off from their church would ultimately achieve a good purpose. God was saying that many will find shelter beneath Brian's branches. The heaviness on his heart immediately lifted—he had just received God's personal assurance.

There is nothing like knowing with absolute certainty that you have just heard God's voice. Although it is usually not audible, it is louder than the booming of a whole bank of thousand watt loudspeakers at a Rolling Stones concert.

Your divine Lover is calling you aside. He is beckoning you to join Him for a romantic rendezvous. If you can sense that He is drawing you, don't let the moment slip by. Now is the time—fall into His loving arms and hear His heart beat—every beat is a beat of pure love for you!

PASSIVE OR ACTIVE GRACE?

"If Allah wills" are the words we often hear from our Muslim friends. This is nothing new—Christians have been heard to say the same about their God. "If it be thy will", are the faith obstructing words of a person who has not discovered what the will of God is. This fatalistic Christian view renders believers' prayers impotent!

Christ has restored to us the dominion that Adam once had. This dominion allows believers to rule and reign over life's challenges. Unless we use our authority, Satan is likely to take the gap. Unless we boldly take authority over his devious plots to trip us up, he will take our passivity as permission to walk all over us. Frankly, unless we know that we have the power to tell Satan where to get off, he won't get off.

When we know the will of God, we can pray in line with it. Faith needs something to hook onto, and the will of God as revealed in the word of God has the loops into which our faith-hooks fit perfectly. When our faith is hooked up to the grace that's recorded in God's word, it is pretty secure.

Peter knew God's will concerning healing; he had read in Isaiah that by His stripes we would be healed[47] and that's why he wrote in one of his letters, that by His stripes we "were" healed (past tense)[6]. Once Jesus had been whipped, it become a fait accompli—all sickness had been dealt with forevermore, and now it is for us to enforce what He accomplished for us.

Peter was so convinced of this, that he was able to speak health to the lame beggar at the Beautiful Gate without making any mention of an addendum of "if it be Thy will". He just told the lame beggar to rise up and walk in Jesus' name[49].

Jesus said that the Father would grant any request made in His name, provided we receive ownership before materialisation by faith[10]. It's not about wait and see—ownership is immediate! Then it is only a matter of time before materialisation takes place.

Quite obviously, we can't exercise this degree of certainty if we are not entirely convinced that by His stripes we "were" definitely healed. It stands to reason that, if we don't know the will of God concerning what we are praying for, we won't have the gumption to be emphatic. Faith is all about being uncompromisingly categorical! Practical faith is not about being of the Christian faith; it is about being convinced that the words we speak in faith carry God's authority! Positive results come to those who believe that their declarations of faith are the final say on the matter[11].

May I hasten to add: There are other kinds of prayer, such as asking for wisdom or direction. Should we move to this city or that? Or should I take this employment or that? These are occasions when we require God's guidance. This is not the type of prayer where we know the will of God. When we need direction and wisdom, we are quite at liberty to ask for it. Even then, immediately upon praying for wisdom, we are required to believe that we have received wisdom. James made it perfectly clear that if we are still in doubt after praying, we simply will not receive what we asked for[88].

When it comes to matters that are indisputably part and parcel of His covenant with us, our prayers need to be emphatic and unwavering. For those who find this kind of praying equivalent to making a servant out of God, they might be missing the point. We are not commanding God to do something; we are commanding circumstances to do something. In other words, we are enforcing the covenant of grace. God gave us dominion and He expects us to use it.

The moment we slip the words "if it be Thy will" into our prayers, we are admitting that we do not know God's will concerning the matter in question. People who are fearful of sticking their necks out in faith, can always slip "if it be Thy will" into their prayers to give themselves a readymade excuse to explain why their prayers didn't get answered. Believe me, this kind of praying will need an excuse. James says that faithless prayers don't get answered, period[88]!

When "if it be Thy will" prayers go unanswered, it can always be explained away by saying that it wasn't God's will in the first place. Sadly, in doing so, God gets blamed for something He did not do. Jesus said, "Most assuredly, I say to you, whatever you ask the Father in My name He will give you" [103]. "Whatever" is pretty all-encompassing, wouldn't you say? We must decide whether He was being truthful when He said "whatever". If we feel religiously compelled to correct Jesus by adding the words "if it be Thy will", we are inferring that He lied to us. From Jesus' words it is clear—He is perfectly okay with us praying for "whatever".

The objection that often pops up when this subject is broached, is that we only have this assurance when we pray in line with His will[134]. I always welcome this objection, because it gives me opportunity to remind them that Spirit led people would never be led to ask for anything outside of His will. Quite obviously, we cannot expect God to join us in doing something sinful. It is not that He tries not to sin; it is that He is incapable of sinning!

The Bible is His word, and His word is His will. We are left in absolutely no doubt whatsoever as to what His will is. For starters, He wishes above all else that we prosper and be in good health[133]. We know without a doubt that prayers in line with these words have His stamp of approval—answering them is cut and dry! We should not be laying blame on Him for unanswered prayer—He doesn't deserve to take the blame when the fault lies with our wishy-washy "if it be Thy will prayers". Wishy washy faith just doesn't cut it with Him!

More than that, He has already decided on the terms of the covenant. We can rest assured that prayers of faith in line with what He has covenanted with us, never go unanswered. All He requires of us is that we ask the Father in Jesus' name. By meeting this requirement, we are assured by no-one less than Jesus, that positive results will follow[103]!

We would do well to leave face saving escape clauses out of our prayers—they serve only to cancel prayers. We don't crumble into defeat when our prayers appear to go unanswered; we crank up our determination! When Daniel prayed, God immediately dispatched the answer to him, but it took twenty-one long days for the angel to get it to Daniel. His progress had been blocked by the powers and principalities of darkness. The angel needed Daniel's unwavering faith. Later, breakthrough came when Michael, the archangel, came to the aid of the angel whose journey had been blocked[106]. The moral of the story is that, before the answer materialises, we should be unflinching in our belief that we gained ownership at the precise moment of our first pray [10]. How long will it take to materialise? How long is a piece of string? If we are determined to stick to our guns for as long as it takes, time will be of no consequence to us.

Grace does not mean that God's love just automatically pilots our lives down the right path, and that we don't have our own steering wheel to point ourselves in a chosen direction. Grace does not make us passive bystanders just watching our lives unfold before us.

God could just as easily have chosen to control us with sheer brute force, but He has chosen to influence us with love, conveying it to us through grace. As with a magnet, His love draws us. But we still have a choice to either ignore His loving advances, or to respond to Him in like manner.

Submitting is enormously enriching! At no cost to us, health, provision, wisdom and direction are ours for the taking. We need Godly direction, not only in spiritual matters, but for every aspect of our day to day living. Let's face it, our daily encounters can always do with a little help. And we find all the help we could ever wish for wrapped in grace. Grace gives us access to a profitable and fulfilling life.

The pursuit of happiness is a shallow quest—long on promises; short on delivery. In this pursuit, we only find happiness when we are better off compared to someone else. The problem is that the moment we achieve our goal, we find others with whom to compare ourselves, and this brings us more discontent. And so the tiresome pursuit continues—it's a vicious circle—there is no end to it.

As wonderful as it is to be happy, God didn't promise us a rose garden. He said that in this life we will encounter trouble, but He didn't leave it at that; He went on to say that He would deliver us out of each and every one of our troubles[51]. If you believe in passive grace, you will leave matters to work their way out on their own. But that is not the Bible way. The very reason that we are required to pray, is to enforce the victory already obtained for us by Jesus.

Truth be told—God doesn't always get His way on earth. This is because He has placed the dominion of the planet into the hands of men[52]. He operates by invitation. That's why, in what we call the "Lord's Prayer", we are instructed to pray, "Thy will be done on earth as it is in heaven."[53] God needs our invitation to do His will on earth. From this instruction it is also clear that grace requires active participation. If we want His intervention, then we need to call for it. It's easy to say that God can do anything, and then just wait and see what He chooses to do, but that is not how we rule and reign together with Christ Jesus.

If you were to argue that God always gets His way, then can you explain why everybody on the Planet is not saved? After all He made it perfectly clear that He is not willing that any should perish, not even one[54]. Millions are dying without Christ every day. Quite clearly, His will is not done unless we play our part. We have been tasked with the mission of enforcing the covenant of grace.

Those who believe grace to be passive will quote that well warn verse that says that everything works together for our good[55]. This is their way of saying that they can just passively stand by and watch things turn from bad to good without making a contribution of emphatic faith. Then when things don't work out in their favour, they can easily explain it away by saying that this additional misfortune will eventually work out for their good. Then when matters finally end up in irreversible disaster, they can still claim that it was God's will for them to suffer.

That is not the context of this verse. The preceding verses talk about praying in the spirit[56]. In other words, all things work together for good when we actively apply the grace that we have been granted. The onus rests with us to team up with the Holy Spirit in prayer.

Then you will find others who will tell you that God causes mishaps for our ultimate benefit. I have never come across an earthly father who would maim or kill his infant daughter for her own good, yet many Christians are maimed or killed in all kinds of mishaps. Can anybody explain to me how a dead child benefits from such tragedy? Quite obviously, tragedy is not how God goes about doing us good. We ought not to blame Him for our own carelessness and mistakes, nor for the unfortunate twists and turns of life.

There is a verse of scripture that says that what the enemy has intended for our harm, God is able to switch to our benefit[57.] Notice that it is not God who intends to harm us, but the enemy. God is the one who undoes what the enemy intends for our harm. Can we benefit from these hurts? Unquestionably! If we remain steadfast in faith in the face of hardship and tragedy, we come out on the other side with reinforced confidence—emboldened to believe for even bigger divine interventions. But we do not automatically benefit from testing—the prize only goes to those who refuse to give up! For example, when we choose to side with the enemy by agreeing that we are sick, our faith does not become stronger, it simply ceases to fight back and surrenders to the sickness. Faith is characterised by dogged perseverance and unshakable endurance—it refuses to give up, even when all the odds are stacked against us[78].

When we choose to say that we are healed, in the face of all the professional medical opinion and physical evidence that says we are not, our five senses will scream out at us in pain, demanding that we come into agreement with our pain and admit that we are sick. We have a choice to make—whose report will we believe? Will it be the doctor's diagnosis, or will it be God's words which state that by His stripes we "were" healed[6]?

The tense of this scripture tells the whole story—"were" is past tense. When we pray, we activate what has already taken place. God does not have to lift a finger—we "were" healed 2000 years ago. All that is left for us to do is to declare health by faith in Jesus' name, and to rest in the knowledge that sickness was defeated by the stripes inflicted upon Jesus. It's a matter of patient expectation—an uncompromising knowing that all is done and dusted! Nothing more is required of God or of us!

Some believers will tell us that we are lying when we say that we are healed, when it is obvious that we are sick. Look at it this way: There are two realities—we must decide which outcome we prefer—it's either the doctor's reality or God's reality. All the medical evidence may be saying that we will die, but the word of God tells us that we "were" healed, and if we "were" healed, then we "are" healed. The choice is simple—what do we want—the sickness that can be seen, or the health divinely endowed upon us?

If Jesus was clear on anything, He was clear on this—He said that we can have whatever we say[11]. We can state present realities, and not have our prayers materialise; or we can state what we desire, and have our desires materialise! Again, the choice is ours. Faith is about emphatic declarations! It is not about wait and see, nor is it about eventually getting possession if per chance our prayers get answered; it is about taking personal ownership of the answers to our prayers before they materialise. Our pattern of speech affirms what we believe.

The choice is yours—you have God's permission to call those things which do not exist as though they do exist[36]. That is how everything was created by Him[35]. He didn't wait for it to begin to get light before declaring that it was light—it was pitch black when He commanded darkness to become light, and we all know the dramatic outcome. That's all well and good for God, you might be thinking, but where does it leave us mortals? Could we even imagine that He would commission us to do something that can't get results[62]? When it comes to creative words, we are in the self-same boat—God's words in our mouths carry His authority when spoken in faith in Jesus' name.

Grace abounds to us for a very good reason, and that reason isn't so that we may sit back and wait for something to happen. God is able to make all grace abound to us, so that we may have sufficient within ourselves to do every good work[58]. Grace is God's way of empowering us to do good works. People motivated by grace, can't help being gracious to others. Grace gives us the power to do what's right. We don't have to be told to do good works—good works appear in our actions, and we have no explanation for it!

PERFECTIONISM A KILLER

"I must be perfect and without fault." If you buy this awful lie, it will drive you to the brink of insanity. Everybody else is aware of their imperfections, and quite frankly, rather happy to discover that you are in the same boat. Perfectionism is disturbing to relaxed people. If religion has convinced you that God requires you to be as holy as God, religion has doomed you to spiritual failure. Thankfully, no one expects perfection from you; least of all God! He doesn't have a single perfect person on His books. He works with what He has, and that's why He chose you and me just as we are. He doesn't even expect us to change ourselves—He has commissioned His Holy Spirit to attend to that. He undertakes this task with gentleness, leading from the front, showing the way forward; never pushy nor confrontational. He could just as easily have bullied us with almightiness but chose not to force holiness upon us. Rather than judge, He chose to love us irrespective of whether we change or not. To discover value in God's sight, is to discover healthy self-esteem, which in turn empowers us to esteem others more highly. Without this healthy self-love we are apt to punish ourselves for failing to be perfect—the awful blight of perfectionism!

Perfectionism is burdensome. It strips the joy out of any task. I watched a friend knitting a jumper. After spending most of the day knitting a sleeve, she noticed a mistake near the start and unravelled the entire sleeve to get to the mistake. For the life of me, I couldn't see the mistake—not even after she had pointed it out. When I said that nobody would notice, she replied that that wasn't the point—while she was aware of it, she simply couldn't allow anybody to wear it. But isn't time too valuable a commodity for such triviality? Once used, it can never be reused.

We are called to excellence; not perfectionism—take care not to confuse the two concepts. Perfectionism is a misguided form of legalism, every bit as deathly as any religious law. Perfectionism says that this is my standard and I dare not perform below it. We get this awful affliction passed down to us by our parents who innocently tell us that if a job is worth doing, it is worth doing well. Nothing wrong with that well-meant adage; unless it gets twisted in our minds to mean, "If I can't do it well, I will not do it at all." That wise old sage, Solomon, said that nothing gets done by people who wait for perfect conditions[89].

The frequency of emails from one of my friends dwindled to a trickle. I hoped I hadn't offended him, but later found out from his wife that it had nothing do with offence—it was just that he was so terribly meticulous about his grammar and spelling that it took him far too long to perfect emails. So, emails stopped because he couldn't find the time to refine them.

Don't you just love emails and SMSs. Spelling and grammar don't count anymore—as long as you can make yourself understood, it's okay. What a shame to allow perfectionism to rob us of the joy of staying in touch.

Have you ever found yourself wanting to do something truly meaningful, but not having sufficient resources to get your idea off the ground? Perfectionism doesn't allow a person to do something unless it can be done properly, and so just never takes off.

There is a verse in the Bible that says that we are not to despise small beginnings[59]. Some of the world's giant corporations had their beginnings in humble kitchens and filthy garages. But, in the mind of the perfectionist, nothing can come of such dismal beginnings. Perfectionism is a dream destroying affliction!

Pride, legalism, religiosity, judgementalism and perfectionism are first cousins, and they are an ugly bunch of relatives with all kinds of evil intentions for those who live by their harsh standards. It's all about competing with fellow believers. Not that superiority is anything worth having—it is a relationship breaker. Outclassing others does not go very far towards winning friends and influencing people.

Religion can be harsh and judgemental towards those, who in its opinion, don't measure up, but fortunately, God's way is different. He doesn't use accusations and judgements to straighten us out; He knows that only unqualified love and acceptance can do that.

Accusations and judgements cause us to be preoccupied with the very things that we are ashamed of, and this preoccupation causes us to do more of what shames us[130]. Thankfully, that's not God's way!

When shame reduces us, we reduce others. It's the knock-on effect known as the "tall poppy syndrome". When we have little value for ourselves, the moment others show any value for themselves, we cut them down to size.

We end up with horrid hang-ups that manifest in nasty retorts such as, "Who does he think he is?" Actually, all he may be thinking is, "God loves me!"

David must have seemed awfully arrogant in his showdown with Goliath. The scene he came upon took him by surprise. Israel's mighty army was cowering at the words of a singular soldier in the enemy's camp. But surely God's people should not be allowing anybody, giant or no giant, to frighten them—God was on their side! David was not shy to voice his disgust.

His brothers were decidedly unimpressed. Who was this pip-squeak of a little brother to make them out to be wimps—they were "men"; he was still wet behind the ears. Who does he think he is? How dare he talk tough as though capable of bringing the giant to his knees. Talk about tall poppy syndrome—his brothers did their best to cut him down to size.

What was it with Israel's mighty men of war? They were armed to the teeth. Besides, they had an enviable track record. There was Moses, Joshua, Gideon and many more—all super conquerors. What was their problem? With God on their side, how could they be cowering before a singular soldier in the enemy's ranks? Yet this insignificant shepherd boy, with no military training, no weapons of warfare, armed only with a harmless looking kiddie's slingshot, was not in the least bit intimidated by his size. But then again, with God on our side, size doesn't count. He approached Goliath oozing with confidence. Listen to the cocky tone of his words, "You come to me with sword, spear and Javelin, but I come to you in the name of the

Lord Almighty—the God of the armies of Israel, whom you have defiled. Today the Lord will conquer you, and I will kill you and cut off your head. And then I will give the dead bodies of your men to the birds and wild animals, and the whole world will know that there is a God in Israel! And everyone will know that the Lord does not need weapons to rescue his people. It is his battle, not ours. The Lord will give you to us!" [32]

"Who does this whippersnapper think he is?" Those who witnessed his unshakable confidence could be excused for mistaking God inspired cockiness for arrogance. But then again, this is perfectly normal for a person who knows that he has the backing of heaven. This is what God's love does for an individual! It inspires unshakable assuredness. And if ever there was anybody who knew he was loved, it was David. His many psalms bear witness to an intimate love relationship with God. What unwavering confidence—it was in direct proportion to his knowledge of God's love for him. Those who discover this degree of love, discover the source of super-confidence.

Somehow religion has got this weird and wonderful idea that our repentance will reward us with more of God's favour, but this idea is not in the Bible. The Bible clearly states that it's the goodness of God that leads to repentance, and not the other way around[15]. In other words, the discovery of His love for us is what changes us. The depth of our repentance is determined by the depth of our understanding of His love for us. When the penny eventually drops, and the un-conditionality of His love becomes clearer to us, we notice that we are behaving differently. Not something we initiated; it's a product of knowing His love!

Sadly, with the influence of religion, we can easily become proud of our achievements, and there is nothing more off-putting than religious puffed up-ness. Conversely, under the influence of God's love, we discover our value, and it is this that gives us permission to love ourselves. In an environment of unconditional love and acceptance, we find ourselves moving from one level of glory to the next—improving without trying—not something for which we can take any credit. But it doesn't stop there; with it comes more trust, more confidence, more faith, more peace of mind and more joy. In a nutshell—a more complete life—Jesus called it abundant life[26]!

WHO IS CHASING WHOM?

Religion has got us on the hop—ever chasing yet never catching. Now my small grandchildren and I are different. Try as they may, they cannot catch grandpa. My artful dodging keeps me just beyond their reach. It's not that I don't want to be caught, it's just that I love hearing their laughter and shrieks of delight. Actually, I can't resist being caught, so I just give in and let them win after a while. That's when I get my chance to gather them into my arms to squeeze my love into them. Then it's my turn to catch them. I could catch them within a stride or two, but I choose to let them get away, and then with very small shuffles, I feign the effort of a fast run, and purposely let them escape my grasp as they squeal with excitement. At first, I resist the temptation to catch them, but eventually relent—it's another opportunity to spin them around and get another hug or two.

At first it's all one sided. I am the only one giving love. It takes a lot of one sided loving and plenty of patient giving, without the slightest hint of reciprocation. But ultimately, love pays off big time!

When one is tiny, so much is taken for granted. What could be better than being a kid? Room service is five star. Everybody is at your beck and call. Mom changes you, feeds you and sings you to sleep. All it takes is a bit of shouting the odds, and breakfast is served.

There is no middle man; breakfast is on tap direct from the dairy—the same goes for lunch and dinner. You don't have to be loving; you just have to be demanding. Returning love comes a little later in life—learnt from seeing relentless love in action. The love that mom gives is unconditional—we get it even when we are intolerably obnoxious. A mother doesn't even notice that her love is not being reciprocated—she just gives and gives unstintingly, way beyond the call of duty.

At first, love is not something that we do; it's something that God does. It takes a lot of unconditional loving from His side before the penny eventually drops and we come to understand how secure we actually are in His love. But a problem arises when we try to earn His love. Religion would have us believe that the chase is all one sided. They insist, "Chase after God with all your might!" But is this really what He wants of us?

If we dare to be honest with ourselves, we must admit that, after a while, chasing after God can be wearisome. We may have difficulty admitting to it, but at the back of our minds is this nagging sense of unfairness—we are not getting a fair return on the effort we are exerting!

We can't help feeling that our faith should be stronger; our walk with God should be closer; our witnessing should be better; our Bible studying should be deeper; our praying should be longer; our service to the church should be more committed, and our giving should be greater. It always seems that we just cannot become what religion requires of us.

How often haven't we heard ministers outlining definite steps that would lead to a more meaningful relationship with God? Sermon after sermon calls for more effort, but we still haven't caught up with the effort outlined in previous sermons. The pastor does his best to get the congregation to aspire to something more meaningful, and judging by the nods and amens, everybody seems to be in agreement. They can't all be wrong, so we fall in with them and try all the harder. Once again we promise ourselves to pray harder, work harder, study harder, give more and sin less—a promise we have never managed to keep for more than a few days.

For those of us who have chased after God, there is always a huge difference between the Christianity we profess and the Christianity we actually experience. We can't help feeling that, despite our dogged chasing after God, we are the ones making all the advances, while God is failing to play His part. Week after weary week, we turn up the wick and put in a little more effort, but always seem to come up short. After a while, there is this sense of exasperation that just won't go away. We get to wonder whether or not we're the only ones feeling this way. Judging by all the smiling faces at church, everybody else seems to be coping with what's expected of them. We get to feel lost in a maze, while everybody else seems to have found their way out. Or could it be that nobody is prepared to admit that they are in the same boat—also frustrated; also performing under par?

Draw near to Him and He will draw near to you, is a scripture that we know so well, but try as we may, we never seem to be able to draw near enough[61]. It's as though He is always just beyond our reach.

I know it is small comfort, but you're not the only one who feels that way. Burnout is a common Christian malady afflicting pastors as much, if not more than anyone else. Doesn't that tell a story all of its own? What is responsible for this religious illness? If this is the best outcome for drawing near to God, then why bother with it? Or could we have misinterpreted "drawing near to God" to mean "doing more stuff for God"? Two entirely different concepts. Should we be drawing near to God? You bet we should! Where are we missing it then? What should we be doing differently? The opposite of frenetic buzzing about, is laid-back relaxation—there is no further obligation upon us except to love as we have been loved. That leaves us with one pleasure, and that is to crumple into His loving embrace and leave the rest to Him!

A pastor friend told me about one of our country's most beloved Bible teachers. He had pastored one of his denomination's largest congregations and been the principal of their national Bible Seminary. This man had spent a lifetime amazing me and others with his profound understanding of deep Bible truths. People would flock to him from near and far just to witness him dissecting God's word in microscopic detail. At the end of a lifetime of service to God, this giant in God's kingdom opened his heart and told of his disillusionment with it all. He seemed to have spent a lifetime chasing after God, and now, tired and worn out, he was wondering if it had been worth the trouble.

If this general in God's army couldn't chase God down, what chance do we have of doing it? This is not only his story—it's the story of so many believers and I don't think I would be wrong if I guessed that it is your story too.

Doesn't it just sound so right to be chasing after God? Religion has got us committed to all kinds of churchified activities in an endless mission to obtain more of God, and it is wearing us out. In a game of tag, we take turns at being "it". Wouldn't it be great if we could stop chasing, and give God a chance to do the chasing?

What, if after all your diligent striving, you were to find out that you've got it the wrong way around and that it is not you, but God who is the chaser? Think back to the day that you gave your life to Jesus. Did it happen because you chased God down, or was it He who chased you down with His love? Consider for a moment—He loved you even though you had done nothing to deserve it.

The truth of the matter is that before you were even born, He had already thought of everything that you would need, and then went out of His way to purchase it for you. In going to the cross, He was well aware that, to buy your health, wealth, peace and happiness, it would cost Him His health, wealth, peace and happiness. He so dearly wanted you but knew that it would take more than mere words to convince you of His love. He weighed up the cost of the pain and humiliation at the hands of lesser mortals. As high as the price was, if it were only to gain your friendship, it would be worth His while. You alone were worth every painful stroke to His back, every flesh tearing nail to His hands and feet, every piercing thorn to His brow, every blasphemous affront to His dignity! Your comfort was more important to Him than the royal comforts that were at His beck and call. Winning your affections were more important to Him than the pain and agony of the cross. Not a single drop of His blood would be wasted, if only to gain your friendship—so desirous is He of your companionship!

He started this love affair without you lifting a finger. Since then, He has never stopped chasing after you—at it every moment of every day. There isn't a second that you are not on His mind; He knows about your every problem. He is with you, wooing you with sweet whispers of love. But it is difficult to hear Him while you are allowing your shame to speak louder than His sweet whispers of affection.

In case you are not entirely convinced about who is chasing who in the divine romance; here's what Jesus had to say on the subject. In the story of a woman having ten coins; He likens Himself to the women and us to the coins. When she loses one, she makes every effort to find it. Note that the coin makes no effort to be found. Here Jesus is actively chasing after us at a time when we have absolutely no interest in being found. How do we explain such committed love? Outlandish, wouldn't you say[119]?

In the story of the shepherd, He leaves ninety-nine sheep to find one that went astray. Here Jesus is the shepherd and we are the lost sheep[120]. Again, it is not we who are chasing after Him, but He who is chasing after us. Even if we have chosen to spurn His love to wander off on our own, He chooses not to be offended by such rejection and just keeps chasing after ungrateful and disrespectful humanity. To my way of thinking, with my limited capacity for tolerance of unappreciative humanity, this kind of unoffended love verges on insanity! This is where I lose it! What kind of love is this? What kind of patience could possibly stretch so far?

In the story of the prodigal son; God is the one who runs towards us, His problem children, and He is the one who forgives without allowing us the slightest opportunity to beg for it—He doesn't even give us a chance to come up with a plausible excuse, much less an apology[14]. One would think that He would demand that we make amends before any thought of forgiveness. But not so with Jesus; He is the chaser in this romance—the passionate suitor in the love affair—the One who does all He can to convince us that He is a suitable marriage partner.

Religion has taught us the reverse, and has got us on the hop, ever chasing the shadowy promises of religion's creation. Like a little puppy caught up in the deception that he will eventually catch his tail if he just runs a little faster in circles; religion sets us off on an impossible tangent to gain God's love—impossible because we already have all of His love! It seems as though nobody is brave enough to stand up and admit that they are exhausted by the futility of it all. Religion's promises are many, but sadly, religion is flawed; powerless to make good on its many promises.

In the book of Revelation, it is not you that is knocking on His door, but He that is knocking on your door[96]. He is doing this at a time when you have grown cold towards Him—you have left Him out in the cold and perhaps even fallen into serious sin. In this picture you are on the run from Him; yet He is running after you and patiently knocking on your door. Why would He pursue a saint that, try as he may, can't stop sinning? Obviously, there is a lot more to His love than meets the eye!

Amazingly, His pursuit of you has nothing to do with your level of Christian service, obedience or sinlessness—it doesn't even have anything to do with your love for God. It's not that He must force Himself to chase after you; it is that He cannot bear the thought of being apart from you. He desires your company and appreciates your love. In as much as we crave human company, so does He. God's whole idea of creating mankind in the first place was for the purpose of fellowshipping with mankind.

If He is so desperate for fellowship, why doesn't He strike up a friendship with the angels? After all, they'll give him a lot less grief. But then again, He doesn't get the same satisfaction from fraternising with the servants[118]. Nothing, but the company of His beloved children can complete Him in His Fatherhood.

In as much as it hurts when our loving advances are shunned, one can only imagine how God must feel when we, in the interests of "holiness", deny His loving advances, calling it "Sloppy Agape". But not even that seems to faze Him—His love towards us doesn't even skip a beat—He just keeps reaching out to us with love and understanding and continues chasing after us regardless!

The most destructive lies are the ones we tell ourselves, and they usually go unchallenged because we keep them to ourselves.

The nymphomaniac who became pregnant after having sexual relations with her dearest friend's husband resorted to abortion. The lie that keeps playing over and over in her head is, "How can God love a worthless whore and child murderer like me?"

The pastor who was caught in a compromising position with the organist, keeps reminding himself of the lie, "The only reason that I am sorry is because I was found out—how could God love a fraud like me?"

The elder who is a secret drinker; the businessman who cheated his trusted partner; the young man who was molested and now lives with identity problems; the single mom who blames herself for her divorce; the kid who cheated in school exams; the boy who betrayed his best friend; the unmarried couple who are living together; the endless bickering of a married couple—we all have our own reasons for believing that we cannot be loved by God. But every reason is nothing but a lie!

We are so busy beating ourselves half to death with shame that we cannot allow ourselves the luxury to believe that we are loved by God. Held hostage by nothing more than falsehood and lies—nothing but religious smoke and mirrors. These lies might be unrealistic, but to us they are real and every bit as tenacious as bulldogs. The only way to break their mighty clench is to confront them with God's unconditional love—the kind of love that says that we don't have to do a thing to change ourselves, because God loves us exactly as we are. He doesn't lay any heavies on us, and doesn't even ask us to make any promises.

"I am so unworthy. I can't help it—I just keep falling back into the same old sins again and again. I am good for nothing!" we tell ourselves. The good news is that, while we define ourselves by what we have done, God doesn't—He defines us by what He has done for us. He is the chaser, remember. His love is gracious enough to look past our sins and love us for who we really are—His beloved children.

In Del Parson's famous painting of Jesus cradling a new born fleecy lamb in His arms, we get a sense of His loving care for the hapless creatures that we are. He left ninety nine sheep to find one pathetic straggler. In this picture, He is anything but angry with the sheep for its thoughtless wanderings. His compassion shines through every stroke of paint on Del Parson's canvas[120].

Del Parson took great pains to find the right man to be the model for the painting of Jesus as the shepherd. Finally he made his decision and took the man of his choice to a farm where he planned to photograph him carrying a lamb across his shoulders. Sadly, the only suitable lamb he could find was ill, unable to hold its head erect long enough to be photographed. After each attempt to position its chin upwards for the photograph, it would simply flop down and droop limply. This was not the image that he had envisaged for the painting.

Eventually they gave up trying, and began packing up to leave. Then, seemingly quite by chance, something magical happened. As Del Parson glanced up, he saw something quite extraordinary. The model, now overcome with deep compassion for the hapless creature, was cradling it sympathetically in his arms. Immediately Del Parson knew that this was exactly the picture of the compassionate Jesus. He was convinced that it was precisely the way that Jesus would want himself to be portrayed on his canvas. The loving way that Jesus deals with His rebellious children was perfectly reflected in the model's deep compassion.

I am sure that you have heard many profound expositions of this wonderful parable. Perhaps you have heard the same fearful version that was told to me. Shepherds would sometimes have to break one of the lamb's legs so that it would stop straying. You may even excuse the infliction of such awful cruelty; applauding it for its ultimate good. But such a harsh thought is entirely out of character with our heavenly Father, and entirely inconsistent with the parable of the prodigal son.

The prodigal was unconditionally accepted, and immediately restored to right standing with his father as though he had never put a foot wrong. His father did not lay down the law, nor did he set any preconditions for restoration. There was no lecture for his waywardness; no threats; no speeches of, "I will let you off this time, but don't push your luck sonny; there will be no mercy next time". Nothing of the sort! This kind of unconditional mercy, love and acceptance runs entirely contrary to that of a leg breaking shepherd.

In being so magnanimous, the prodigal's father risked giving his deepest love to someone who could just as easily fall back into his old sinful ways, as stay faithful to his dad. What kind of love would cause a person to expose himself to this kind of vulnerability? When it comes to His beloved children, God is never short on love. In granting it so freely, He makes Himself vulnerable to the possibility of being rejected and taken advantage of—even so, He is willing to risk it all on you!

In case you feel that you have fallen too far to identify with a cuddly little new born lamb, the lost sheep was probably not the lovable creature that we have been led to believe it to be; it may have been a gnarly old stubborn ram with crooked horns and muddy wool—dishevelled and matted with thorny brambles. This is a more true to life portrayal of the mess that we often get ourselves into. We are often weary, worn out by life's unfair twists and turns. Are you finding it easier to identify with such a sorry creature? If so, don't despair; no matter how bedraggled you are, God's love for you is relentless, chasing you down with mercy, favour and grace!

There is nothing more satisfying than to stop running and to just allow yourself to be caught. This is when He gathers you up into His arms, spins you around and squeezes His love into you!

THE PERFECT RELATIONSHIP

As a teenager, as one might expect, I embarked on the exciting adventure called courting, without the faintest idea of what it was all about. With little experience, intimate liaison had little chance of surviving. Truth be told, even after years of marriage, I still hadn't figured out the true meaning of love's give and take.

Would I be right in saying, everybody starts out as apprentices—experimenting, floundering, learning what love is not before discovering what it is. Through a process of what can be bitter trial and error, we eventually stumble upon what true love is. The same cannot be said for every relationship—some never discover its true meaning, settling for something more akin to manipulation or lust, rather than selfless love.

We may try to woo a partner with our wit, but wit can so easily turn to sarcasm. We may try showering our partner with gifts, but true love cannot be purchased. We may try wooing with our wealth, prowess or macho-ness, but end up being overbearing and controlling. Our beauty may attract, but inevitably, what lies beneath our attractiveness soon shows through—beauty is frivolous; only skin deep.

Not everybody learns anything from the lessons that lead to marital bliss. Half of all marriages flounder and drown in the rough and tumble of misunderstandings. Others end up with marriages of convenience; still others agree to put up with each other for the sake of the kids. The nature of some marriages is that of master and servant, as one party domineers the other. Still others barely survive the destructive waves of jealousy and mistrust.

Jesus wants us to be His life's partners, but He will not settle for anything less than a "marriage made in heaven". He cannot afford to attract us with His gifts and end up with a marriage that is based on our infatuation of His things. He wants to be infatuated for all the right reasons. So many religious movements revolve around the premise of getting things from God. I assure you, God does give good things to us, but if we're in the relationship for His things, all He has from us are purchased hearts, and there is no romance in that. He is looking for real relationships, not for convenient arrangements. In adding conditions, we would be reducing romance to no more than a commercial deal, a gazillion miles short of the love He desires to shower upon us.

Nor can He afford to force us into an arranged marriage and have us cowering as though He is an overbearing tyrant. He dearly wants to give and receive affection, and the only way to know if affection is genuine, is if we have the liberty to either accept or reject His loving advances.

Instead of forcing us to bow to His almightiness, He allows us the freedom to choose either to love or not love. He is determined to win us over with nothing more than love. He wants to be wanted for all the right reasons—He wants love; not religion, and He is prepared to pursue us until we are convinced of His noble intentions.

We don't easily give our hearts to another, especially when pressured to do so. But when our hearts are captured by unconditional love and acceptance—well now, that is an entirely different matter! God has wired us to respond well to love, and to see manipulation for what it is.

Lovers cannot bear the thought of being apart for more than a moment—they crave each other's company. Feelings for one another cannot be purchased, nor can any amount of surreptitious pressure cause them to feel the way they do about each other—nothing but true love can arouse such emotions.

God has no hidden agenda. He is not interested in a shotgun marriage. Although, in His almightiness, He could easily force us into a relationship, yet He chooses to romance us with unbridled love. What does He desire in return? Nothing but our romance!

Religion is not at all happy with such freedom. After all, what if it leads to wrong decisions. Religion must interfere and help us out—it must be prescriptive and dictatorial. Unfortunately, religion's many requirements have a way of dampening the thrill of spontaneous affection—ingredients essential to romance.

One denominational stream may offer a relationship with God's things rather than with a heavenly lover, but no price is high enough for true love. Another stream may offer a relationship with a God who is so high and mighty that intimacy would be most unlikely. Still other denominations offer relationships of slavish servanthood, but God does not fraternise with the servants. Then there are those who would offer a relationship with a law giver, but God's emotions are not touched by what we can boastfully say we have or have not done. Then there are those who would offer a "clergy-go-between" relationship, but a messenger cannot convey the depths of our love for each other—it requires intimacy. Jesus is not looking for a pen-pal; He is looking for a real live lover. The go-between version—the doctrine that elevates clergy above laity—the doctrine of the Nicolaitans, is the version that Jesus specifically singles out as the one that He "hates"[18].

None of the versions offered by religion can satisfy God's deep need to love and be loved. We are not loved because of anything that we have done or not done; we are loved because we were created to be God's companions—someone with whom He can share His glory—someone to lavish love upon.

If heaven and hell were not a reality, would you still want a relationship with God? If your answer is yes, what reason would you offer to convince others of the benefits of such a relationship? Remember that you cannot scare them with the flames of eternal punishment nor lure them with the promise of a harp and a cloud. Your answer will reveal a lot about the type of relationship you have with God. Is it really His love that keeps you close to Him, or is it simply a free passage to heaven, an escape ticket from hell? No matter what shallow reason you may have for your relationship with Him, you can rediscover His passion for you. Before long, His deep love for you will rekindle your love for Him.

Maybe you are one who was initially attracted by His love, but perhaps, as time went by, religion slowly but surely convinced you that a relationship with God is something that is awesome and fearful. Let's face it, love does not fare well in the environment of overbearingness and trepidation. Anything that puts distance into romance ruins intimacy—sweet nothings cannot be whispered into each other's hearts from a distance.

Or perhaps religion told you about God's things, and before you knew it, the seduction of the glitter of those things outshone the romance. It may have happened gradually, but before you realised it, the excitement of love had already faded. No matter what caused the cooling of your once raging passion, what you once had, can be rekindled. All it takes is a rediscovery of the depths of His love for you!

So often when we hear the story of our divine Lover, He is portrayed as a holy prosecutor. But is He our dreaded prosecutor or our loving defender? He cannot be both. We must make up our minds on this. Unless we are thoroughly convinced that His love cannot in the slightest way be influenced by what we have done or not done, we will be susceptible to religion's often warped view of God's impeccable character.

Unlike His love, our love for Him is seldom without limits. But our boundaries are progressively enlarged as we progressively discover the depths of His love for us! His love knows no limits—loving us despite our many failings and shortcomings! As hard as it is to admit, we often disappoint Him, yet His love just keeps on coming. Jesus is saying, "So many people live in dread of Me, because they have never heard My story told the way it should be told.

"They hear about My omniscience, and that leads them to believe that I am all knowing and therefore know all their secret sins. This causes them to avoid Me.

"Others hear that I am omnipotent, and that causes them to think that I will use my all-powerfulness to crush them when they sin, and that too becomes a reason to avoid Me.

"Then there are those who have heard about My omnipresence, and they conclude that I am present everywhere so that they have nowhere to hide, and that also becomes a reason to avoid Me.

"They cannot imagine that My omniscience translates into their wisdom; My omnipresence translates into My constant loving companionship, and My omnipotence translates into their personal authority and power!

"They have heard of My law, and that becomes a reason to fear Me. They cannot imagine that I have fulfilled the law on their behalf and provided grace and mercy for their many failings[2].

"They have heard of the curse of the law, and that becomes another reason to fear Me. They cannot imagine that I became a curse for them so that they would no longer be cursed[3].

"They have heard that I am the alpha and omega,[65] the beginning and the end, and that becomes a reason to fear Me, because they fear that I may use My almightiness to dominate them with tyranny. They may see Me as a despot who is accountable to no-one. They cannot comprehend that My unshakable love for them provides them with unshakable dependability.

"They have heard that I am holy and that they are not. They cannot imagine that I have shared My holiness with them for no other reason than that I desperately crave their company. All that I ask of them is that they believe in Me[66]. I will give them as much time as they need to fall in love with Me. They don't have to promise to fix their failings for My sake; change will take care of itself as romance blossoms. My passion will arouse their passion."

"They cower at My glory, and My glory becomes another reason for them to fear Me—they cannot imagine that I want them to have my glory in their lives." [67]

If one were to ask ten people to describe God, one is likely to get ten different descriptions. They can't all be right. The truth is that each and every person's perception of God is closely aligned to that of their Bible mentor's. Nothing wrong with that—unless, of course, our mentors' ideas of grace have been distorted by tradition. Regardless of whether perceptions run true to reality or not, they are innocently passed on from generation to generation, and continue in the same innocent way to be passed on by us.

A friend of mine was sorting through his late father's papers when he came across a portrait photo of his dad. It was so badly damaged with age that his father was barely recognisable. As much as he wanted to frame the picture, he felt that its tattered condition would not do justice to his dad's dignity.

As he contemplated how best to restore it, God showed him that he needed to restore another image—the image that he had formed of His heavenly Dad. What he had perceived of God was far from the reality of who He actually is. Religion had given him a twisted image of God's loving character, and this had resulted in an awkward relationship with Him.

Religion has given many of us an inaccurate picture of God, consequently, we relate to a god that is less than the God of grace—almost as if worshiping a foreign god.

We don't question our perspectives. If we see Him as our prosecutor, then we will have a defendant/prosecutor relationship with God. Obviously prosecutors don't fraternise with defendants, and so an intimate relationship is most unlikely.

To some extent, it is true to say that the character of our God is a creation of our imagination, and if we get His character wrong in our thinking, we could be worshiping vastly different gods. Those who see Him as a holy thug will not experience the same relationship as those who know Him to be a caring Father who relates to His children with infinite patience, love and understanding. Our perceptions determine whether or not a divine romance is possible.

The story of God's love is the most beautiful story ever told, but with the passing down from one generation to the next, it gradually changed until it became the scariest story ever told. Many evangelists have turned it into a story of escaping hell's torment, when it should be the story of a king who became a pauper in order to find a bride. Incognito he searched. He didn't want a bride that would be overwhelmed with his majesty—he wanted a genuine romance that would develop naturally for all the right reasons. He wanted a bride that would love him, not for His wealth, but for who He is.

Yes, He would share His majesty with His bride, but that had to be secondary to romance! He could not afford to have us bought by the thought of being exalted to royalty and showered with jewellery.

The liberating story of God's faithfulness, in spite of our unfaithfulness, has over time evolved into a fearful story of God's judgement of our unfaithfulness. Paul was determined to know nothing except Christ Jesus and Him crucified[68]. Paul came to a point in his life where he finally understood that his achievements were not the issue—the real issue was what the blood of Jesus had achieved—His blood was enough! Paul did his level best to convince us that we are no longer condemned, not because we no longer sin, but because we are in Christ. The fear, shame and uncertainty that came to us through Adam's sin was brought to an abrupt and decisive end with the blood of Jesus.

The Old Covenant had to be put aside so that the New Covenant could take effect[69]. If the Old Covenant had not been put aside, it would have required us to run very hard to keep a lot of law just to stay in God's good books. And there would have been a hefty price to pay for breaking its many rules[70].

Fortunately, under the New Covenant, the onus is not on us to keep covenant—our end of the deal has fallen squarely on Jesus' shoulders. He has undertaken full responsibility for keeping our end right!

If God were to renege on only one promise, He would immediately be unholy—covenant breakers cannot claim to be holy! But thankfully, our God is unquestionably holy, and therefore incapable of breaking a covenant. If it were not for His holiness, He would be vulnerable to being overthrown. No need for concern! You're safe with Jesus—He is not a covenant breaker[71].

The New Covenant is not the only covenant for which God took full responsibility for keeping both ends of the deal. When He made covenant with Abraham, He put Abraham to sleep so that he would not foul things up with words of doubt and unbelief[72]. In Abraham's absence, God effectively cut covenant with Himself, and therefore the responsibility for keeping Abraham's side of the deal would not lie with Abraham; it would lie with God.

Here is the good news—Abraham's covenant has become our covenant[73]. Abraham was the wealthiest, most blessed individual, on the Planet. As usual, it is Jesus who made it possible for us to enjoy what was promised to Abraham. He did this by becoming a curse in our stead so that the blessing of Abraham becomes the blessing of every Tom, Dick and Harry. All that is needed is to receive it by faith[3]. Here too, Jesus took full responsibility—He knew that in our hands the covenant would soon be botched. With this awesome responsibility resting squarely on Jesus' shoulders, we can rest assured that it is infinitely more dependable than it would have been had it rested on our shoulders. Our shaky resolve to keep promises would wreck the covenant in a heartbeat, thus nullifying God's obligations to us.

This marvellous relationship is not about our faithfulness; it's all about His faithfulness. It's not about our strength; it's all about His strength. It's not about our ability; it's all about His ability. He has promised to stay in relationship with us forever[75]. When we are unfaithful; He remains faithful[76]. Although it is a given; despite our most ardent efforts to not slip up, as sure as God made little green apples, we are going to slip up—of that there is no question. Let's be honest! Sin is not something that we want to do, but it is something that we are going to do. Even so, we remain righteous in His sight. That's because we stand in His righteousness; not our own[77]! When we fail Him; He doesn't fail us. God is well aware that our resolve to stay faithful is like the cool early morning mist that evaporates with the first hint of sunshine.

When He made a covenant with Abraham and his seed, He personally ensured that it would be unbreakable, and that is why it remains perfectly intact to this day—not dependent upon our purity, and therefore without regard for our many deficiencies. If it were dependant on our purity, it would be a leaky boat held together with nothing more than spit and chewing-gum.

Abraham was counted righteous, although in practical terms he was anything but righteous, and the same goes for us[31]. He walked in the blessing of the covenant; not in the blessing of his personal purity, and it's the same for us. We simply cannot take any credit for being chosen to be blessed; God did it all by Himself, and His favour is available to us merely for believing!

WE ARE PERFECTLY UNDERSTOOD

I am often taken aback to discover that people I have only known on the phone, bear little resemblance in the flesh to the image I have formed of them in my mind. We subconsciously associate a voice with height, weight, attractiveness, ethnicity and age. Our delusion is exposed when we meet the person in the flesh.

In other ways, we are often inclined to believe myths concerning each other. We may imagine somebody to be an intellectual and feel that we do not measure up sufficiently to get into discussion with them. Or we may see somebody as being very wealthy, and this may cause us to feel too outclassed to befriend them. Of course, none of this may be true, so we end up relating to a myth rather than to reality.

Sometimes the myths that others believe about us are convenient smokescreens, and we prefer it that way. Sadly, when this happens, relationships are often contrived and artificial. We may prefer to have the inflated opinion of others, no matter how untrue. We may think, "If they really knew the truth about me, they wouldn't like me anymore."

Imagine if you were to make public your most awful thoughts of: revenge, lust, anger, irritation, impatience, bitterness, improper fantasies—how many friends would you be left with?

How refreshing it is to find a true friend who knows our inappropriate thoughts, quirks and oddities, and yet accepts us for who we are. Jesus is such a friend. He knows everything about us—our best and our worst—our conniving, our manipulating, our selfish motives—nothing is hidden from Him; yet He loves us regardless!

The One before whom we will one day stand, knows our most dreadful hidden secrets—all the dark places of our hearts—the most embarrassing details that haunt us. No amount of grandiose puffing up of ourselves can possibly impress Him. He knows us for who we really are, yet despite this, He is still madly in love with us. Our nasty blemishes and our gnarly warts and unsightly thoughts, though socially inappropriate and sometimes even grossly offensive, yet He chooses not to be offended! How do we explain such faithful devotion? It's beyond reason! Thank God for His Grace! It trumps sin[128]!

One of the great intellectuals of the nineteenth century, Friedrich Nietzsche, was also one of history's most outspoken atheists. He dedicated much of his life to disproving that God exists. What had convinced him?

Nietzsche lost his father at a young age and was raised by a matronly family of Bible-bashing Christian fundamentalists. Under their severe discipline, he was taught about a wrathful god who rules with iron-fisted rage and who judges without empathy— a holy tyrant—a divine despot! It comes as no surprise that, with the passing of time, he would grow to despise and reject that god.

He used his outstanding brilliance to cast doubt on all belief in God. His anti-Christian writings and lectures are legendry. He set out to convince the world of the absolute foolhardiness of believing in God.

Ironically, we should feel the same way about that god. Like Nietzsche, we should be every bit as dedicated as he was to obliterate that god from the minds of believers, because, quite clearly, that god is not the God of the Bible—the God of the Bible is the God of love, mercy and grace!

When we understand what caused Friedrich Nietzsche to reject his family's religion, we ought to applaud him. He intuitively understood the foolishness of following such a god. How could he be expected to love a tyrant? He was convinced that the universe was too well balanced to be ruled by an unbalanced despot, something we simply cannot deny!

Regretfully, many believers have not come to Nietzsche's conclusion. They have bought into religion's ideas. Too many have come to accept that God is capable of wild mood swings, as if an unbalanced schizophrenic! They see their relationship with Him teetering on a knife's edge—as though He is an unpredictable bully—one moment a loving father, and the next a stern judge without empathy. They are convinced that His moods are influenced by how well or otherwise they have behaved. They see him as a revengeful record keeper, a stern judge and harsh dispenser of retribution.

What chance is there of gaining the approval of a vengeful god who knows our darkest thoughts and meanest sins. Can we ever be sure of where we stand with him? I very much doubt it! There is no point in trying to impress a god who is erratic and unpredictable.

Friedrich Nietzsche never heard the true story of a gracious God from his family, and consequently came to despise the god they had portrayed to him in word and deed. Church goers who have come to know the god Nietzsche knew, are likely to live in fear of that god's touchiness and volatility. Who can blame them for rejecting him altogether? They do well to do so! More than that, they ought to be congratulated!

Despite our unfaithfulness and tendency to sin, God has chosen to love us unconditionally. How do we explain such glorious madness? This kind of gracious generosity is way beyond rationality!

There is a question for which nobody seems to have an answer: "If we're so troublesome, why does God bother with us?"

Will we ever come to understand how completely infatuated God is with us? Seeing that nothing about us is hidden from Him; how is it possible that He is still so wildly in love with us?

At times, we may be irritated by the behaviour of others. But have we taken the trouble to understand the underlying causes for their quirky behaviour? We weren't there when their uncle molested them, or when their parent's split up and left them damaged by rejection.

We forget that, if we were given the same dreadful set of circumstances, we would in all likelihood be just as irksome to others.

We don't always cut enough slack to irritating attention grabbing people, but God does. He understands the dynamics that establish low self-esteem and self-destructive inferiority complexes. The very thing that infuriates us about a person, escapes His notice—He is blinded by the brightness of their righteousness in Christ. Despite our penchant for sin, He finds in us something immensely appealing. Like parents who refuse to hear anything bad about their children, so it is with our God and Father[132].

Sometimes our loudest accusers are fellow occupants of pulpits and pews. Often chorusing religious accusations, while finger wagging and head shaking their disapproval in perfect unison with that other snake in the grass, better known as "the accuser of the brethren". But there is one who never has a bad word to say about us—in fact He has forgotten that we ever sinned[82]. And His name is God!

CONCLUSION

Religion has got it wrong! Being a Christian is not a matter of behaving better; it's a case of extreme heart makeover! Jesus didn't come to do a touch up job; He came to transform us into the god-class of being; the kind that shares His Father's unconditional love, His righteousness, His glory and His favour!

Next comes the extreme "home" makeover. He demolished the Old Testament Courthouse with all its charges stacked against us, and in its place constructed a magnificent love nest.

As the crowds of angelic beings stand chanting, "Move that bus! Move that bus! Move that bus!" the bus slowly pulls forward, to reveal a breathtakingly beautiful place of extreme love and acceptance, where there is no place for personal guilt, remorse or shame.

The lingering shame that you may be feeling in God's presence will soon be soothed away as you relax in Papa's loving embrace. He will never let you go—graciously choosing not to notice your sins[82].

As your bridegroom lifts your veil and gazes lovingly into your eyes, He is enthralled with your beauty. He exclaims in wonder, "My darling you are so desirable and perfect in every respect."

You have come home to a place of rest, where chasing God is a thing of the past. Instead of continuing with your breathless chasing; you relax in His loving arms.

"This is all well and good" I hear you say, "But why don't I feel loved?" That is a question you should be asking of religion. If you have been relating to a god that is a mythical construction of religion's imagination, then you have every right to be feeling unloved—you have been defrauded!

You cannot experience true freedom until you are prepared to lay down all feelings of guilt and inadequacy, but you can't do that before you have been awakened to God's unconditional love and acceptance!

The truth finally dawns upon us—God's love really has no strings attached. His unconditional acceptance of us gives us ample reason to accept ourselves. And with self-acceptance, we have nothing further to prove. Without persuasion, we find ourselves loving others—it seems to come naturally. When the depth of His love awakens our love, accusations from religious voices fall on deaf ears.

The greatest crime of our age is not serial raping and killing, not even the terrorism that destroyed the lives of thousands of innocent moms and dads on 9/11. The greatest crime of our age is the lie that religion is God's idea! For as long as we fall for this lie, we will have a form of godliness that denies the power thereof[38].

Litmus paper turns red when dipped into acid, and blue when dipped into alkaline. God's love story is your litmus paper—use it to test your divine romance. You will soon discover that a relationship characterised by manipulation and legalism fails the test, but a relationship characterised by mercy and grace passes the test with flying colours!

Religious rulership often lends legitimacy to manipulative mind games. Under the beady eye of legalistic monitoring, what chance is there of our actions being shaped by God's love? Holiness cannot be legislated; it wilts and dies in the poison of legalism, but blossoms and blooms in the nourishment of spontaneous love. Under religion's misguided rulership, God ordained individuality is unceremoniously snuffed out—sacrificed on the altar of denominational conformity!

Don't for one moment imagine that religion can be fine-tuned and tweaked into a state of grace. If you are serious about switching to grace, are you prepared to eradicate every last vestige of legalism from your relationship with God? Grace is completely opposite to legalism—the two cannot co-exist in the same person. The one casts aspersions, while the other liberates!

At first, minds steeped in religion are not able to fully grasp something that is so enormously liberating—it takes a process of pulling down every thought that dares to exalt itself above the knowledge of God[79]. What is the knowledge of God concerning you? You are exceedingly desirable to Him—He is smitten, and love struck with you—besotted and enamoured! Are you ready to be loved in such a complete way?

If you are still not convinced that grace is your friend and legalism your foe, then I have failed you. I must accept that I am not convincing enough. I beg of you to reconsider. A life more loved awaits you—a life of greater possibilities—a life elevated above the bondage of shame!

Dear reader,
I will never leave you nor forsake you[75].
With all my love,

God

REFERENCES

1	Phil 3:19	38	2 Tim 3:5
2	Matt 5:17	39	Luke 10:30-37
3	Gal 3:13	40	Eph 5:25
4	Matt 19:29	41	John 3:16
5	Gal 3:1-3	42	John 8:3-11
6	1 Pet 2:24	43	Heb 8:13
7	2 Cor 8:9	44	Luke 23:43
8	John 15:16	45	Acts 2:21
9	Matt 7:7	46	Psa 16:11
10	Mark 11:24	47	Isai 53:5
11	Mark 11:23	48	Mat 7:12
12	Matt 16:19	49	Acts 3:2-11
13	John 19:30	50	Eph 1:22
14	Luke 15:11-32	51	Psa 34:19
15	Rom 2:4	52	Amos 3:7
16	Luke 7:47	53	Matt 6:10
17	Eph 3:17-18	54	2 Peter 3:9
18	Rev 2:6	55	Rom 8:28
19	Mark 9:35	56	Rom 8:26
20	1 Cor 13:12	57	Gen 50:20
21	Rom 7:8	58	2 Cor 9:8
22	Psa 105:15	59	Zech 4:10
23	Heb 11:31	60	Matt 10:41
24	Matt 1:2 & 6	61	James 4:8
25	Matt 26:70-74	62	1Cor 11:1
26	John 10:10	63	1 John 4:18
27	Matt 23:9	64	Rom 6:18
28	Luke 10:38-42	65	Rev 1:8
29	Matt 5:27-28	66	1 Cor 1:30
30	Heb 4:3	67	John 17:22
31	James 2:23	68	1 Cor 2:2
32	1 Sam 17:45-47	69	Heb 10:9
33	1 John 1:8	70	Deut 28:1-68
34	Matt 6:1	71	Num 23:19
35	Gen 1:3-28	72	Gen 15:12
36	Rom 4:17	73	Gal 3:14
37	1 Cor 13:8	74	Luke 6:32-33

REFERENCES

—

75	Heb 13:5	107	Psa 66:18
76	2 Tim 2:13	108	Gen 3:9
77	2 Cor 5:21	109	Matt 6:12
78	James 1:4	110	Rev 1:5
79	2 Cor 10:5	111	Psa 37:25
80	John 12:47	112	Mark 8:22-26
81	Jer 23:3	113	Prov 23:7
82	Heb 8:12	114	1John 4:8
83	Rom 3:27	115	Rom 6:1-2
84	Phil 1:21	116	Rom 8:32
85	Eph 3:20	117	Rom 8:17
86	Author unknown	118	Heb 1:14
87	Matt 26:6-13	119	Luke 15:8-10
88	James 1:5-8	120	Luke 15: 4:7
89	Eccl 11:4	121	Gal 2:21
90	Luke 7:28	122	2 Cor 5:21
91	Eph 4:8	123	Heb 10:12
92	Ezek 17:22-23	124	Rom 8:1
93	1 Thes 5:17	125	John 14:9
94	Luke 6:45	126	Acts 17:28
95	Luke 10:27	127	1 John 4:17
96	Rev 3:20	128	Rom 5:20
97	Matt 6:33	129	John 13:17
98	Luke 11:5-7	130	1 Cor 15:56
99	1 John 3:9	131	Gal 5:6
100	1 John 2:1	132	2 Cor 5:19
101	Jer 31:34	133	3 John 1:2
102	Rom 3:22	134	1 John 5:14
103	John 16:23	135	Isai 64:6
104	Lev 19:19	136	Matt 11:6
105	John 8:11	137	Eph 3:19
106	Dan 10:12-13	138	Psa 56:11

Deon and Susan Stevens

I believe that Deon is a strategic champion of a Glorious Grace revolution taking place throughout the earth. This is not a book of empty froth, bubbles and shadows but it has the substance of rich unveiled truth unfolding in a supernatural sequence of liberating revelation that will set your heart racing with joy and inspire a fresh love for Jesus. All things are possible to a people set free from uncertainty, confusion and condemnation. Thank you so much Deon for your courage and compassion. I honor you and salute you in His abundant Grace.

Rob Rufus, Pastor of City Church International Hong Kong.

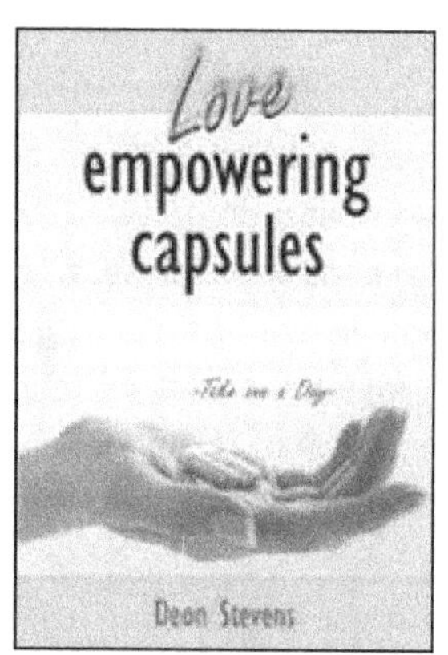

Believing in God's grace is one thing—a wonderful idea in theory but how do we apply it to our daily lives? Where did we get the idea that God is a small-minded bookkeeper, tallying up our failures and successes on a score sheet?

How you score in life has no bearing on the degree of grace you receive. We are the objects of God's furious love pursuit and we can luxuriate in this liberating knowledge.

If Christians are guilty of anything, it would be navel gazing. So much time is spent with self-introspection, self-recrimination and self-condemnation. Somehow, we have lost sight of the fact that we are made right because of what Jesus did and not because of what we did. Love Empowering Capsules brings our perspective back to our privileged position of dearly loved children who are fully empowered to lead overcoming and abundant lives brimming with peace and joy.

If you have inherited so much in Christ, why would you continue striving so hard to get it?

He left you wealth, health, peace, joy and much more—yet you may not have experienced this. Your inheritance did not come to you because of your good works or holiness and therefore cannot be taken away because of your lack thereof. If you insist on working for it, there aren't enough hours in the day for you to do enough to deserve it. You are already in receipt of an immense fortune. Continuing to strive for it is ludicrous. Your bountiful inheritance was placed into your personal trust account so that you can withdraw from it at your pleasure. It's already yours—why in the world would you still be striving to get it?

When you discover how highly God esteems you, exactly as you are right now, your self-esteem will get a shot in the arm, boosting your sense of worthiness to appropriate His favour. You are not highly favoured because you are holy but simply because you are His dearly loved child.

Grace, the most treasured gift of all, is under fire from a most unlikely foe—Christendom itself. Grace is often perceived to be at odds with holiness. But it takes more than good intentions to achieve holiness—it takes love. Holiness is love in action, and we have no better example of it than in God's grace. Sadly, when Christendom reduces grace, it reduces our redemption.

"In Christ", we are so much more than mere mortals. In reality, we have what Christ has! This knowledge opens the door to enormous possibilities. Although the price has been paid in full, we may have to make some mind adjustments before benefiting from the payment. If we were to discover that religion is holding us back from God's best, would we be prepared to walk away from it?

Fulfilment in life—the ultimate prize! It is something that one would expect to find in religion. After all, religion makes many claims. But these claims are often beyond our reach. They are only obtainable through the often maligned, gift of grace.

Jesus is not the founder of a religion; He opposes religion. He made His feelings patently clear—He did not appreciate religiosity—never uttering a single word of accusation to sinful humanity, but never having a single kind word for religious people. Oodles of fulfilment can be found in grace! Feelings of inferiority and self-doubt simply cannot survive its edification. It inspires faith and godliness, and makes life enormously fulfilling!